Swedish Carving Techniques

COLUMBIA COLLEGE
674.88S958S
SW

S0-ADF-147

3 2711 00004 5179

MAY

ENTERED DEC 7 1990

Swedish Carving Techniques

Wille Sundqvist

Translated by
James Rudström

The Taunton Press

Library of Congress Cataloging-in-Publication Data

Sundqvist, Wille.
   [Talja med kniv och yxa.   English]
   Swedish carving techniques / Wille Sundqvist ; translated by James Rudström.
      p.   cm.
   Translation of: Talja med kniv och yxa.
   Includes bibliographical references.
   ISBN 0-942391-45-4 : $15.95
   1. Wood-carving—Sweden—Technique.   2. Wood-carving—Sweden—
Equipment and supplies.   I. Title.   II. Series.
TT199.7.S8613   1990   89-40574
   ᵃ.88—dc20   CIP

674.88 S958s

Sundqvist, Wille.

Swedish carving techniques

Front cover photo: Jögge Sundqvist
Back cover photo: Gunnel Sundqvist
Photos by Wille Sundqvist and Jögge Sundqvist, except as follows:
pp. 56-62, 64: Rick Mastelli
pp. 104-106: Birgitta Rudström

©1990 by The Taunton Press, Inc.
All rights reserved

First printing: February 1990

First published in Sweden by
LTs förlag
S-105 33 Stockholm
SWEDEN

Printed in the United States of America

The Taunton Press
63 South Main Street
P.O. Box 5506
Newtown, Conn. 06470-5506

Translator's Note

On a cold, dark October evening in 1973, I ran out of sandpaper while working on a sailboat in my shop. The stores were closed, but across the street a light was shining from the Handcrafts Consultant's office. Knowing little of what that meant, but hoping the word "handcrafts" would lead me to sandpaper, I ventured across the street, was let in and there met Wille Sundqvist.

Little did I realize then that Wille would be my guide for years to come, introducing me not only to traditional Swedish handcrafts, but also to the subtleties of the knife and ax. Wille teaches how to use these essential hand tools, but more than that, he teaches design through them. A simple wooden spoon becomes a carefully engineered object, refined through generations of innovation. The spoon integrates material, form and function, taking shape to the rhythms of the knife and ax.

I recall once hearing, "That guy must have built that shack with an ax," in other words, crudely. But the intricate detail, yet harmonious simplicity, of spoons, ladles and dough bowls made by knife and ax has forever abolished my misconceptions about these tools.

Production woodworking, with or without machines, has forced the craftsman to work from straight reference surfaces—face sides and face edges. To produce curved surfaces, the wood must first be made into rectangular shapes. This is necessary in production, yes, but in traditional applications the shape of an object is sought out in a tree. A curved stem for a boat's bow can be found in the curve of a tree where the trunk meets the roots. Wille takes this idea one step further. Beyond finding a spoon in the tree, he lets the selected blank dictate the spoon's final shape through its own peculiarities.

Working side by side with Wille to translate this book into English, I discovered that the thoughts and techniques presented here are not the end result of learning and experience, but rather they are part of an ongoing process. This is what makes Wille's book unique. During the course of translating and editing, both Wille and I stayed close to our tools, experimenting, discussing and learning. Our new discoveries became part of this translation.

Skilled use of the knife and ax is seldom described today because there are few persons who master these tools. Those who do are often more articulate with their hands than with words. Wille's words will lead you through the concepts and techniques of the knife and ax. Your practice will lead to woodworking rewards not possible with machines. Wille gives these tools a future, opening the door to further refinements in technique and creative solutions in design.

—*James Rudström*
Vilhelmina, Sweden

Foreword

My experience with carving is rooted in my very early years in my grandparents' kitchen. My grandfather's workbench was there, and it was there my brother and I often sat whittling toys and other important things. In later years I have often pondered the fact that never once did I hear my grandmother complain about the chips and shavings we left behind on the kitchen floor.

During our busy days in the woods cutting timber, we would discover crooked pieces of wood, burls and the like. These were gathered and carefully stored as material for the things needed in our household. The long evenings of fall and winter would give us time to transform these pieces of wood into useful objects.

At the age of twelve, I started carving horses out of the curly wood of willow. A year later, two of my carved horses won honorable mention at a crafts exhibit. Provincial Governor Rosèn presented me with the award in the amount of five crowns, along with an additional five crowns from his own pocket. That exhilarating experience spurred my interest in wood carving.

After innumerable detours, I made my way to Carl Malmsten, the furniture designer, at his school in Stockholm. This proved to be the start of a lifelong relationship with Malmsten. I have him to thank for encouraging rather than ridding me of my natural use of the knife. I completed my formal education as a manual-arts teacher at his school and later taught there. I also had the pleasure of being an instructor at many summer workshops at Capella Gården, the school Carl Malmsten founded on the island of Öland.

For the past 18 years I held the position of Provincial Handcrafts Consultant in the province of Västerbotten. In fulfilling the need for guidance and education in traditional handcrafts, I helped those who depended, sometimes exclusively, on crafts for a living, and promoted general participation in handcrafts. I also initiated workshops on making spoons, bowls and dough bowls with hand tools.

I have come to recognize that there is an enormous lack of understanding and skill in using hand tools—knives and axes in particular. This, along with a realization of the close relationship between hand tools and the keen sense of design that was our forefathers', has prompted me to write this book.

I hope this book conveys to you and to future generations what I learned from my father and grandfathers and from my own discoveries. I would like for others to be able to take part in a common social and cultural tradition through handcrafts. Learning and working together is of inestimable value. Naturally, this is important for our young people, but it is also of great value for others, regardless of age or sex. The change of pace in making things by hand also affords relaxation to those whose daily work is stressful. Beyond that, the things you make are of lasting value.

I would like to extend my warm thanks to The National Association of Swedish Handcraft Societies for granting a stipend, enabling me to take a leave of absence from my ordinary work to get this book together. I thank my son, Jögge, for spending time in his workshop helping me with the photography. I extend my appreciation to craftsmen Sven Hansson of Åsele and Thure Sandström of Vännäs, and to my wife, Gunnel, for standing by my side and lending a hand while I worked on this book. I also give thanks to the Great Father Above, for giving me the strength to accomplish the task of writing this book.

—Wille Sundqvist

Contents

Introduction

This book lends itself to the amateur craftsman interested in carving as a hobby, as well as to craftsmen dependent on handcrafts for a living. It is also suitable as a textbook for manual-arts teachers who wish to reintroduce the use of the knife in manual arts and industrial arts. It can be used as a textbook for study circles and workshops, and for the further education of those leading such groups. This book is meant to stimulate enjoyable and creative activity. Work with a knife can also aid in physical and psychological therapy.

The instructions here are extensive, with an abundance of illustrative material. You should read the text thoroughly and study the illustrations carefully. With practice, you will be able to master the knife grips and strokes and enjoy working creatively. Awareness of your work will lead to an understanding of tool care, materials and design. While you're at it, you will be able to make useful, beautiful things for yourself and for others.

I want to encourage you to consider learning to work with a knife in a group, such as a study circle or workshop. The main advantage is that people can learn from each other. Each individual has personal experience and understanding that can be shared. Directions concerning knife grips and strokes can be interpreted differently by different persons. Putting your heads together will help you to come up with the best solutions to problems. There may be members of the group who know other carving techniques or ways to care for tools that aren't dealt with in this book. These alternatives will lay the groundwork for discussion and will be to everyone's advantage. Working together also stimulates personal creativity. The variety of designs your group will produce will make you all the more conscious of how good design interacts with function, and increase the satisfaction of making small and simple everyday things.

The material covered in this book is basic, but it covers a broad span, and it would take a long workshop or a series of study circles to exhaust the subject. You might go through the book quickly as a group, then each of you practice on your own to master the skills and techniques. The time devoted to each phase will be dictated by the duration of your workshop or the number of times your circle will meet. An experienced instructor, of course, will be of great help in deciding which sections of the book should be covered more intensely. But a study circle without an instructor can effectively organize itself around its own needs and interests. Visits from accomplished craftspeople and trips to museums and crafts shops can supplement this book.

Historical Background

Probably one of our first implements or tools was a stone used to pound or hit something. A handle would make the stone more effective. To fit the handle, it was necessary to shape the stone, and another stone had to be employed. Stone chips were produced, and they could be used as cutting tools and scrapers. The first stone knife was probably made from one of those chips. It is also likely that the first stone ax evolved from the stone club.

The knife and ax are tools that humans have used for thousands of years for innumerable tasks. Although the knife and ax were undoubtedly indispensable as weapons, I will not attempt to cover that subject. For me, the knife and ax are tools to work with, not weapons.

There is a saying in Faeroese: "The knifeless man is a lifeless man." It is difficult to overestimate the importance of the knife and ax. In times past, they were often the only tools humans had to clear the forest for growing crops, build shelters and make implements and other necessities. Hunting and fishing were sometimes more important than agriculture for human survival. Without the knife and ax, such food gathering would have been impossible.

Among the Lapps, the custom of bearing and using knives is an inherent part of their culture, probably more so than in any other ethnic group. The Lapp and the knife are inseparable, at work as well as at play. Often two or three knives hang from their belts: the smaller knives for making repairs, skinning and eating and the larger used in place of a hatchet. The rich ornamentation on Lappish tools and implements are engraved using only the knife, and tell the story of their cultural heritage.

Meals and the knife—From time immemorial, the knife has been used as a tool for eating. Because the knife was always carried, it was always at hand. Women bore knives on a belt or in their pocket or purse. Even at festivities, everyone had a utensil to eat with—the knife. It wasn't until the 18th century that it became fashionable among the upper classes to use tableware of some kind. Common people, however, continued to eat with the knife throughout most of the 19th century. As a child, I can remember the butter knife often missing from the butter. My father was so accustomed to eating with his knife in the logging shack or in the field that when the butter knife got into his hand, it stayed there.

The guilds and education—During the course of a few hundred years, the guilds maintained a protective and very sharp distinction between the trades. Tradespeople were proud of their work, and were much respected for their skill and knowledge. In Sweden, the guilds were officially abolished in 1846 because, with the advent of the industrial revolution, they inhibited competition. In spite of that, the guild attitude has continued in some trades. Furniture makers, for instance, identify themselves with their tools. The chisel means to them what the knife means to common people. This attitude has long endured in schools for furniture makers. During my formal education to become a journeyman furniture maker (a prerequisite for becoming a manual-arts teacher), I often encountered a disdainful attitude toward knives. As the story goes, when a respectable journeyman laid his eyes on a knife, he picked it up with two sticks, with which he removed it from the shop. Thus he demonstrated his disrespect for the knife, not wanting even to touch one to be rid of it.

The Mora knife—The industrial revolution put an end to knife-making on a small scale. Knife production was taken over by manufacturers. In Sweden, the centers for manufacturing knives were in the towns of Mora and Eskilstuna, and the greatest number of knife manufacturers were located in Mora. The best-known manufacturers include Carl Andersson, C.M. Matsson, Mora Knivfabrik, Bröderna Jönsson, K.J. Eriksson and Erik Frost. Of these manufacturers, only the last three are still in existence, and Bröderna Jönsson is the smallest of the three.

Why Use Knives and Axes?

From my childhood, I recall when the men would sit down in the woods, chat for a while and rest from the hard work of felling timber. Someone would always pick up a stick and carve on it during the course of the conversation. When they were done talking, the stick was usually thrown away. The carving did not seem to be a goal in itself, but it seemed to make the conversation more relaxed.

At one time, the kitchen was the room that was kept warmest, and it was there that people spent the most time, making and repairing things. The women carded wool, spun yarn, wove and knitted. The men made utensils and other implements for the household and the farm. For the most part, this sort of close, familial productivity is a thing of the past. Because of the modern, sterile and well-polished standards of today's homes, making dust and shavings or putting a chopping block in the middle of the floor is not acceptable. Woodworkers are not allowed to practice their craft in the house, only in the garage or basement. I have met active and enthusiastic woodworkers, even professionals, who do all their work in a mere six square feet in front of the basement furnace.

Those who work with fiber and fabric are allowed to practice their craft in the home and to enjoy the company of others at the same time. Why shouldn't the woodworker who carves be able pursue his interest likewise? To use a knife and ax, you don't need a special place to house yourself. The ax requires a chopping block, but it doesn't take much room. Why not carve on the living-room sofa? I do that often. I also feel that carvers should be able to take their work with them when they visit their friends or sit in public places. I even carve when I am traveling on the train.

The living-room couch and the train coach do demand that you have a cloth apron to catch the shavings in. You need to practice carving in such a manner that at least most of the shavings really do land in the apron. It's important that we carvers who like to take our work along with us clean up any mess we make, to gain the confidence of people in public places.

Quiet and clean tools—The selection of large and small machines on the market for the woodworker is enormous. Manufacturers try to outdo each other in producing the most ingenious motorized machines. If you happen to own a bandsaw, table saw, jointer or even a few accessories for your little electric drill, you will undoubtedly need a special room or shop to work in. Machines are noisy, so you will need protection for your ears and for anyone else's ears who happens to be close by. Conversation will be made impossible while the machines are running. They also make dust, and it won't be long before you will need a shop vac or a dust-extraction system. But you will still have dust in your shop, and it will find its way into the house.

One thing special about the knife is that it does its work so quietly. The ax makes a little noise—how much depends on how you use it. But I don't hesitate to call these tools quiet when I compare them to electric machines like the table saw. Knives and axes do make chips and shavings, but not dust, letting you breathe clean air and making cleanup easy.

When it is peaceful and quiet, using the knife will not break the tranquillity. Sometimes there will be other things to listen to, such as conversation, music, the singing of the birds or the wind rushing through the leaves. Indeed, sometimes you will listen to the actual quietness around you when you carve.

Training dexterity—Many young people don't get enough practice using their hands, and thus don't strengthen them or achieve much dexterity. If you look closely when they work with their hands, you will see that they lack strength, which is a prerequisite for doing good hand work.

Logical, practical and creative thinking would be of little use if we could not perform the tasks generated by that thinking. It is the hand's skill, coordinated with thought, that has advanced our technical culture to where it is today.

When everything was made and done at home, children had to help with the chores at a very early age. The heavy work of the day and the necessity of producing things for use in the household developed and coordinated the muscles of their hands in a natural way. Through physical education and manual-arts training, today's schools try to fill the gap left by the lack of such training in the home. Unfortunately, schools offer far less than what is necessary for young people to develop skills with their hands.

Even small children like to carve. Soft wood and a sharp knife are prerequisites for their success. My son Jögge, at age four-and-a-half, is carving thick pine bark.

Children are usually fascinated with carving. If they carve regularly, they will surely increase their strength and dexterity. The youngest carvers will need close assistance and the right size knife to fit their hands. But the younger they are, the faster they will learn.

The handcrafts movement—Toward the end of the 19th century, the knowledge of handcrafts and craftsmanship diminished with the advent of machine production. In Sweden, the problem was recognized at an early stage, and the Rural Economy Associations employed handcraft consultants in a few provinces. Local handcraft societies came into existence, and in 1912 The National Association of Swedish Handcraft Societies was founded. Their resources were small, but through great effort and enthusiasm, traditional crafts and work methods were revived.

Fiber and fabric have dominated the handcrafts movement. Until the 1960s, almost all of the handcraft consultants in the country, with a few exceptions, had received an education in fiber and fabric. At the end of the 1970s, there were only four consultants who had backgrounds in materials other than fiber and fabric. At present there are two consultants in Lappish crafts and fifteen consultants in wood, metal and leather crafts. Several of these consultants hold only half-time positions.

Particleboard and souvenir culture—As a result of policies of profit, it is next to impossible to buy kitchen cabinets made of solid wood with glued joints and strong dovetailed drawers, in spite of the fact that we have a well-developed machine technology to aid us. In a couple of decades, these enticing and seemingly stable shelves, cabinets and bureaus found in our furniture stores will be reduced to particleboard rubble in our dumps.

During the past 40 to 60 years, stores and gift shops have come to offer a surplus of machine-made knickknacks and utensils. These products are a far cry from the household articles made by our forefathers. They lack feeling for the materials, design and function. Some of these products have even found their way into handcraft stores in Sweden. What worries me most is that the majority of producers and customers don't think there is anything wrong with these articles.

Even with the versatility of the equipment available, it is difficult for our best woodworkers to achieve all that distinguishes traditional design. Sometimes it is the technical knowledge that is wanting, sometimes it is skill, but often it is a combination of the two. I'm not opposed to machines and other technical aids, and I have even helped woodworkers find ways to finance their equipment. I also realize that often there must be a compromise between design and the machine. What does concern me is how easy it is to fall into the trap of letting machines and production methods dictate design. Design should be ours to decide; machines should help us to do what we want.

Carving and design—Carving something with a knife or an ax is a very tangible way to get a sense of design. Because the object being made doesn't have to be secured in any way, it's easy to move it to different positions and see its lines and shape grow out of the blank. A three-dimensional object isn't just a picture. It's an infinite number of pictures, and all of the pictures must find harmony within the object. The lines of the object must compose one unit, congruent from whatever direction it is seen. Carving teaches design.

Cultural values at stake—Only a generation ago, skill with and knowledge of knives and axes were common. Where is this skill and knowledge today? How many young people can use a knife even to sharpen a pencil? But it isn't difficult to understand why the situation is so bleak. With one exception, no manual-arts shop I've walked into in the past 20 years was equipped with knives suitable for carving—not even the teachers owned suitable knives. Forget a sharp hewing ax and a chopping block. This being the case, it's no wonder why skills in traditional crafts are in decline. The use of the knife, ax and other hand tools, an important part of our cultural heritage, is about to be lost in only two generations.

This is a development to be avoided. Carving has a wide appeal. It doesn't require an exclusive commitment, a special shop or expensive equipment. People like to work with their hands, and they need to do so to increase their strength and train dexterity. Carving increases sensitivity for design and brings forth creativity. Carved utensils and other objects are a joy to use and to live with. They are the lasting result of meaningful work. Beyond this, carving is a way to have fun together. It is my hope that the benefits offered by carving will help to preserve this important part of our cultural heritage. I am optimistic that there is still a chance to pass the art of carving on to future generations.

Tool
Basics

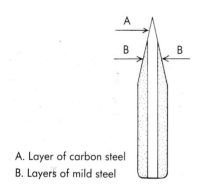

A. Layer of carbon steel
B. Layers of mild steel

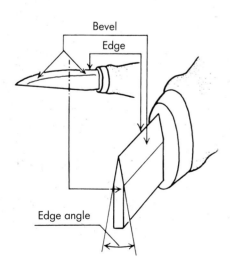

Bevel

Edge

Edge angle

Knives There are special knives for special purposes, knives for carving and whittling, kitchen knives, table knives, hunting knives, shoemaker knives, pen knives, throwing knives and daggers. You might say that most knives are general purpose because they can perform a multitude of tasks. I think this is the reason that the general-purpose knife, or Mora knife, has replaced the older Swedish carving knife *(taljkniv)*. Mora is simply the town in Sweden where most of the knives were once manufactured. Through the years, Mora knives have been made in a variety of sizes and shapes. During the first part of this century, the Mora knife usually had a blade that was 10cm to 12cm (4 in. to 4¾ in.) long, with a handle 10cm to 11cm (4 in. to 4⅜ in.) in length. The handle was traditionally painted a reddish-rust color. The sheath was made of compressed pasteboard that extended far up on the handle, and it had a stitched seam all the way up the backside.

Mora knives have long been an important part of the Swedish household, used to fulfill cutting and scraping needs in the kitchen, in the shop and anywhere else in the house or around the farm. The fact that these knives are so common is probably why they have come into use as carving knives. Most people didn't have, or even know of, specialized knives for carving wood, so the Mora knife was used for that purpose. Through experimentation, a multitude of grips and strokes were developed. These carving techniques make use of the entire blade, sometimes employing the full length of the cutting edge in a single stroke.

At first, the Mora knife may seem long and unwieldy, and not suitable as a carving knife. But by learning the proper grips and strokes, you will discover the versatility of this knife. It will allow you to waste wood fast, shape blanks into usable objects and finish them with smoothness and detail.

Laminated or solid-steel blades—The most important thing for a knife is that it cut well, which means not only that you can get it razor sharp, but also that it will stay sharp. There are basically two kinds of Mora-knife blades: laminated steel and solid steel. Solid-steel blades have become more common in recent years because they are cheaper to manufacture than laminated blades. Solid-steel blades can be tempered throughout to a uniform hardness. This makes them tough, and they can take a great deal of hard use, but it is also their greatest disadvantage. Tempering makes the blade very difficult to grind and sharpen.

Laminated blades, on the other hand, are easy to grind. They have only a thin layer of tempered steel sandwiched between two layers of mild steel. At first glance, a laminated blade may seem to be one solid piece of steel. If, however, you look closely at the bevel, you will notice a seam just above the edge, running along the entire length of the bevel. The middle layer is the somewhat shinier carbon steel below the seam, and this is the cutting edge. Seen in section, the blade would look as it does in the drawing on the facing page. In the photo below, the laminated knives, with a seam in the bevel and shiny steel below it, are easily discernible.

Occasionally I hear someone say that laminated knives are softer toward the back of the blade. This is not usually the case, but it could happen if the blade was unevenly tempered. Solid-steel knives could

A seam on the bevel reveals a laminated blade. The knife in the middle, with no seam, is of solid steel.

just as easily be softer toward the back of the blade for the same reason. On hand-forged blades, the temper is sometimes drawn toward the back of the blade to give it more resilience.

Mora knives are found in a great variety of models made by different manufacturers. They are marketed in North America as sloyd knives, Swedish sloyd knives, Swedish carving knives or universal knives. The only difference between sloyd knives and carving knives is the shape of the blade. Carving knives usually have narrow blades with straight backs; sloyd knives have wider blades with dropped tips. Most of the Mora knives on the North American market have laminated blades and are manufactured by Frost's Knivfabrik AB in Mora, Sweden. The knife pictured at right on the following page is available with a blade length of 82mm (3¼ in.) or 95mm (3¾ in.). It is offered with a traditional tapered handle that is oval in section or with a molded plastic handle. I prefer the wooden handle. Blades are available if you wish to make your own handle (see Sources of Supply, p. 135).

A large general-purpose knife with a solid-steel blade, willow-root handle and stiff sheath of partially tanned leather.

Handmade general-purpose knives and sheaths with curly birch and reindeer-horn handles.

Two Mora knives with traditional sheaths of compressed pasteboard.

Sloyd and carving knives—My first knife was a medium-sized Mora knife. In some cases, it is preferred over the narrower, more pointed carving knife. This is especially true when roughing out blanks. When carving in tight spots, the long blade will necessitate choking up on it, leaving only one or two fingers on the handle.

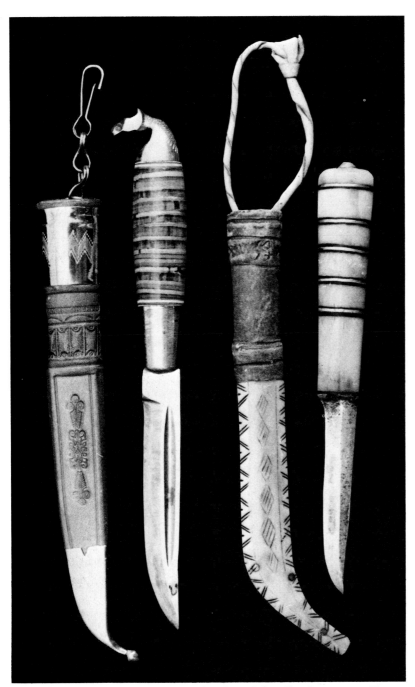

A manufactured Finnish knife and sheath with handle of compressed layers of leather (left), and a Northern Lappish knife and sheath of reindeer-horn, birch bark and leather (right).

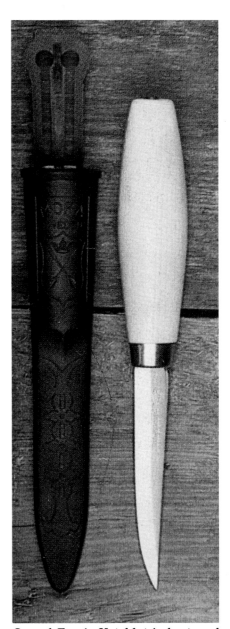

One of Frost's Knivfabric's laminated carving knives with a traditional wooden handle and a plastic sheath.

Grinding and honing will decrease the length and width of the blade; it becomes narrower and more pointed and thus more suitable for close carving. A narrow, pointed blade more easily carves concave surfaces. It's a good idea to have a rounded edge line at the tip of the knife to keep the tip from becoming too thin and fragile. Short-bladed knives, bought that way or ground until they become so, are excellent for carving detail and small objects. Blades as short as 30mm to 40mm (1³⁄₁₆ in. to 1⁹⁄₁₆ in.) with widths of 6mm to 10mm (¼ in. to ⅜ in.) are fine for intricate work. New blades of the Mora type are available in lengths between 70mm (2¾ in.) and 120mm (4¾ in.), with widths between 15mm (⅝ in.) and 25mm (1 in.). Blades wider than 25mm are hard to work with. Blade thickness varies with the size of the blade, but usually will be 2mm to 3mm (⁵⁄₆₄ in. to ⅛ in.).

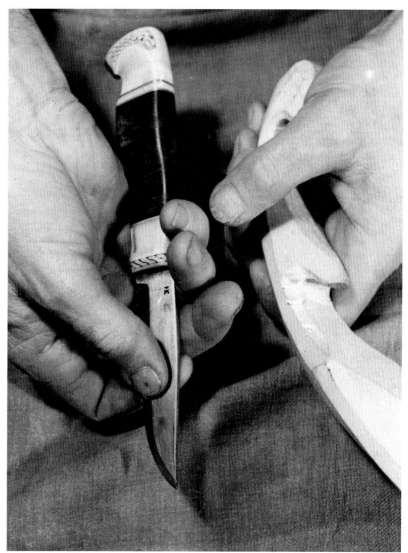

Intricate carving can also be done with a large knife by choking up on it and using only the blade's tip.

These Mora knives have been ground many times. The two knives at left have an excellent shape for carving small objects and getting into tight spots.

General-purpose knives—Many people believe that general-purpose knives should not be expensive, because a knife used every day will wear out or get lost. I feel that something you use often should be of good quality. After all, it's the durability and design that determine if the knife is serviceable or not. Most Lappish knives are good general-purpose knives, whether their handles and sheaths are made of horn, wood, leather or combinations of these materials. The fact that Lappish knives have become works of art through their good design and fine ornamentation does not make them any less usable.

Knife Handles
During the past few years, the interest in making knives for private use or for sale has greatly increased. I have seen many examples of good functional knives, but unfortunately I have also seen many with handles that were too straight, too thick or just plain unwieldy. Then, too, I have studied the complicated and arty ones—they were even less usable than the thick and straight-handled knives. Good design should be functional. You've missed the mark if you carve a handle with a fancy shape and lines that don't work.

Straight handles—Straight handles don't have any brakes, and your hand can easily slip toward the blade or off the butt. If you compensate by making the handle thick to fit a large hand, it will be too thick at the hilt and get in your way. Judging from the wear on the blade, the top knife in the photo below must have done its work, in spite of what I have said.

Handles tapered toward the blade—The knives pictured at right are skillfully made with hand-forged, laminated blades. With handles tapering toward the blade, these knives give you an excellent grip when cutting from the hilt toward the tip of the blade. However, the risk of your hand slipping onto the blade when powering the knife from tip to hilt is obvious. In this case, the only brake will be the friction between your hand and the handle.

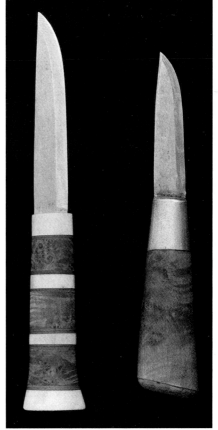

Two well-crafted knives with handles that taper toward the blade.

Straight handles provide little protection against slippage.

Handles that taper in both directions keep your hand in place.

A straight-handled knife with a flared butt (top). Handles that lock in their sheaths need flared butts to grip when unsheathing them.

Tapered handles — Tapered handles, oval in section, are excellent for carving. The thicker part of the handle fits well into the concave part of the hand, and gives the longer middle fingers a good grip on the knife. Because the handle is narrow close to the blade, it gives you the clearance you need to carve close to the blank. The taper toward both ends of the handle lets you get a better grip with both your index finger and your little finger. This safety feature helps to keep your hand from sliding off the butt of the handle or slipping toward the blade. It is a traditional shape with soft and pleasant lines.

Flared butts — Handles with flared butts give you an especially good grip when you are carving from the hilt toward the tip of the blade. These handles will permit you to carve vigorously, using the forehand grip or the chest-lever grip.

The knife pictured at the top of the facing page seems unwieldy. Its handle has no taper toward the butt to keep the hand from sliding onto the blade, and little taper toward the blade leaves no clearance for work close to the blank.

A flared butt is necessary on knives with sheaths that lock onto the handle. These knives lock into the sheath because the leather at the opening stretches around and then tightens past the thickest part of the handle. The knife makes a pleasant "click" as you sheath it, when the hilt contacts the wooden or horn part of the sheath inside. The flare gives you something to grasp when you unsheathe the knife.

Dropped butts — The slight downward bend on the handle of the little knife below keeps the knife from turning in the hand. This bend, though slight, fits the hand well and feels good in all positions. The abrupt taper toward the butt gives the little finger a good grip.

This knife is very functional, and I like its shape. Notice the tension between the contour of the back of the handle and the belly. Seen from above, it has a steep taper toward both the butt and the blade.

Kniv-Kaj's knife — The knife in the photo at right was made by Kaj Embretsen. I have taken the liberty of changing the shape of the handle somewhat, and also roughening its surface to make it less apt to slip. It now has a combination of good qualities: it tapers toward both ends, it has a dropped butt, it is flared on the butt and there is an ever-so-slight flare just short of the hilt. You can feel that the flare is there, but it stays out of the way when you are carving.

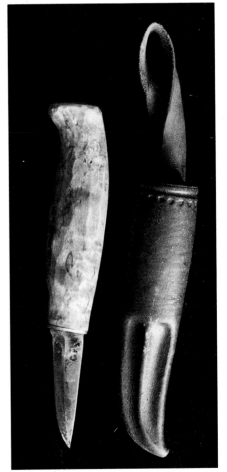

The carved surface of the handle on this knife gives it a good grip. The handle also has a dropped butt and slight flare toward the blade.

An old knife with a beautifully tapered handle and a slightly dropped butt.

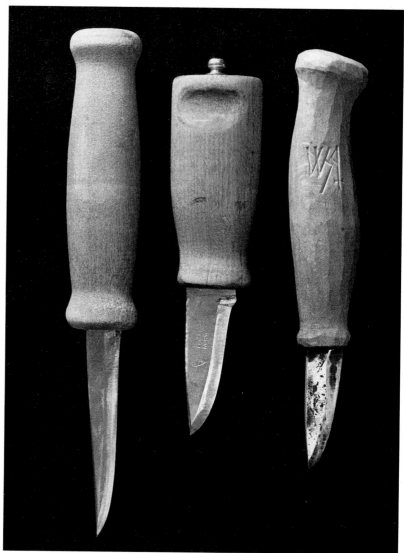

Knives flared at both ends of their handles.

A finger guard is good only when you stab a knife into something.

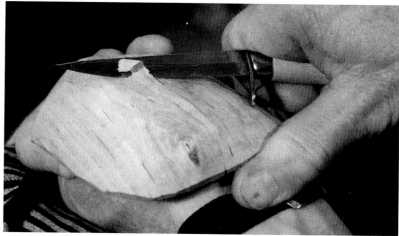

For the carver, the finger guard is always in the way.

Flared toward the blade—A few knife makers make knives with a more-or-less pronounced flare toward the blade. The first knife in the photo on the facing page is often used by those who carve Dalecarlia horses (carved, hand-painted horses from the province of Dalecarlia, Sweden). Of the knives pictured, this knife has the most pronounced flare, which keeps your fingers from slipping. I find it gets in the way, though, especially when carving wide, convex surfaces.

The Norwegian Fjording knife in the middle of the photo is easier to work with, but it does have some drawbacks. The main one is that the handle is too short, and therefore hard to get a grip on. I have made a notch on either side of the handle to give me a better grip on it and make the knife easier to unsheathe. The third knife has only a slight flare toward the blade, but it gives you protection from slipping and stays clear of the blank. Notice the smooth transition from the flare on the butt to the handle proper. This helps to make the knife feel good in your hand, however you grasp it.

Finger guards—The question often arises whether a finger guard makes sense. A finger guard is probably good if you are going to jab the point of the knife straight into something, such as a piece of wood. Most daggers have them for this reason. But they are not recommended for doing traditional carving. The guards are continually in the way and make some grips and strokes impossible. It is not toward the tip of the knife where you have the most power when carving; it is close to the hilt.

Make a Knife Handle   Knife handles can
be made in many ways. Here is one easy method to fit a blade to a handle. First, you need a Swedish-type knife blade, preferably a laminated one (see Sources of Supply, p. 135).

For your knife-handle blank, choose a piece of wood approximately 260mm to 300mm (10 in. to 12 in.) long, 35mm (1⅜ in.) wide and 14mm (⅝ in.) thick. Plane one side of the blank carefully, and crosscut the blank in half. You will now have two 130mm to 150mm (5 in. to 6 in.) pieces, each with a face side.

Position the blade's tang and a part of its blade flat on the surface of one of the blank halves. If you prefer a shorter blade on your knife, just move the blank farther up on the blade (see the drawing below). Keeping the blade centered on the blank half, scribe the outline of the

End view

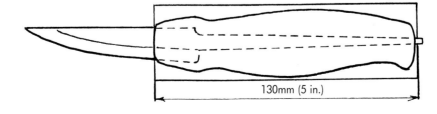
130mm (5 in.)

End view

blade and tang. Saw off the blank about 3mm (⅛ in.) shorter than the length of the tang, and leave the tang proud of the handle's butt. Cut the other half of the blank to the same length. Now use a narrow chisel to cut a mortise to the scribe lines you made on the first blank half. The depth of the mortise should be equal to the thickness of the blade and tang.

As a safety precaution and to protect the blade, cover the part of the blade that will not be mortised with masking tape or electrical tape. Fit the blade in its mortise and position the other blank half to see that the blade is seated properly. Glue the halves together with white or yellow glue. Align them carefully, and make certain they don't slide out of position when you clamp them.

After the glue has dried, clamp the blade in a vise, handle upright and resting on the jaws of the vise. Peen the end of the tang with a ball-peen hammer. You can rough out the handle shape with a coping saw. The final shape can be carved, or shaped with rasps and files. You can finish the handle by coating it with boiled linseed oil, or even better, let it soak in the oil overnight.

Other Carving Tools

To hollow the bowls of spoons and ladles, it is necessary to have either a carving hook or a gouge. In my home, we used only carving hooks to hollow the bowls of spoons and ladles. These hooks were hand forged and very nice to work with. Good carving hools became hard to find, and I have never been able to work well with manufactured double-edged hooks. Thus I started using gouges to hollow out spoon bowls. I have developed a special technique that allows me to work safely with gouges without having to make use of holdfasts or vises. This technique is explained further on p. 116.

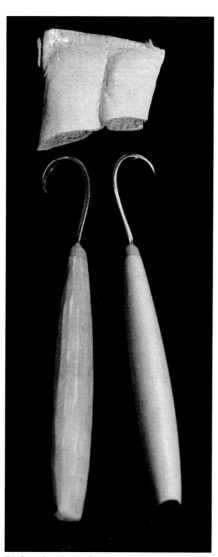

Left-edged and right-edged carving hooks (spoon knives) with their sheath.

Carving hooks—It wasn't until the middle of the 1970s that I once again became friends with the carving hook, after trying the hooks made by Ernst Bergström in Ramsele, Sweden. The curve of his carving hooks makes it easy to remove ridges and unevenness on the flatter areas at the bottom of the bowl. His hooks are single edged, either right edged or left edged. The knife with the edge on the left when the handle is toward you and the hook is turned upward, is called left-edged. The opposite applies if the edge is on the right. Using different grips, a right-handed person uses both the right-edged and left-edged hook in his right hand, and vice versa for a left-handed person. These hooks, correctly ground with a flat bevel, are a pleasure to work with.

Carving hooks, or spoon knives *(skedknivar),* are traditional tools with many variations and many different names. In the province of Väster-botten there are at least two names for them. Close to the Baltic Coast they are called spoon irons *(skedjärn),* and inland toward the mountains they are known as cutting scissors *(skärsax).* The Lapps have a variation of the carving hook that is similar to a scorp. The hook forms a complete circle with a straight tang mounted in a long handle. A leather strap is fastened to the iron just below the handle. The strap has a loop that is pulled over the head and onto the neck. Thus the upper body is used to pull through strokes. This tool is often used to hollow burls that will become bowls.

Gouges—Gouges, either straight or bent, are fine for hollowing the bowls of spoons and ladles. I would suggest getting at least two gouges with different curvatures or sweeps. They should be 12mm to 25mm (½ in. to 1 in.) wide. The drawing at right illustrates a No. 8 sweep, which is good for roughing out the bowl of a spoon or ladle, and a No. 5 sweep, which is used for removing the ridges left by the roughing gouge.

Gouge sweeps

No. 8

No. 5

Straight gouges, bent gouges and bent-spoon gouges are readily available in various sweeps and widths (see Sources of Supply, p. 134). Straight gouges and bent gouges have long flutes; spoon gouges have short flutes that flare out from a thin stem, hence they resemble spoons. Bent gouges are made with a great variety of bends along the flute. Through different combinations of sweep, width and bend, they are quite versatile. Spoon gouges with a dog leg in the stem are very good for getting into tight spots in deep bowls and scoops. Unfortunately, these are nearly impossible to find on the market and must be custom made or bent by a blacksmith.

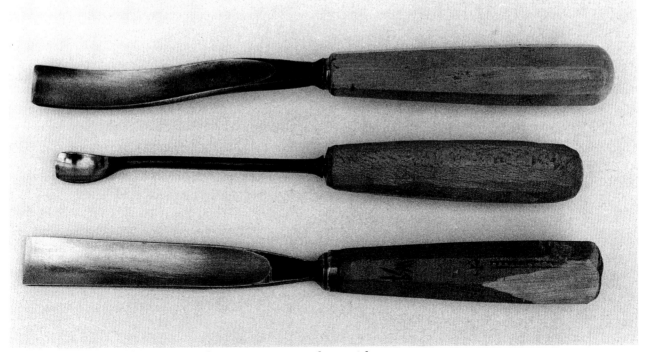

From top to bottom: a bent gouge, a bent spoon gouge and a straight gouge.

Engraving knives—It is possible to use an ordinary carving knife to do fine chip carving to incise letters, numbers and other ornamentation. To do this, you will have to hold the blade between the thumb and the index finger, and guide the tip of the knife without using the handle. Essentially, you are choking up on the knife and holding it like a pencil. Grasping an unprotected blade can be awkward. It is therefore better to make a short-bladed knife and handle solely for engraving. It is important to have the right steel for the blade; a good source is a worn out metal-cutting blade. Be sure to use the part of the blade nearest the teeth for the cutting edge. Most modern metal-cutting blades are bimetal (a narrow strip of hard metal alloy is fused to a mild steel back), and you want to use the hard steel.

Make the blade 10mm to 15mm ($\frac{3}{8}$ in. to $\frac{5}{8}$ in.) long. If you are going to do mostly straight-line carving, the edge should be straight, with a fairly obtuse angle, as shown in the drawing at left. For carving curved lines, the rounded blade is preferable. The edge angle should be the same as for the carving knife, and the bevel should be flat. Shape the handle with a slight flare close to the blade to give you a good grip on the knife.

Drawknives and splitting knives—Knives with handles on both ends can be very effective for shaping and smoothing large surfaces because they permit you to work with both hands. To use them, however, you must have some way to clamp and support the blank. Drawknives (double-handled knives with a bevel on one side and the handles angled toward the user) are uncommon in Sweden. I think the reason for this is the disappearance of the shaving horse in this

Engraving-knife blades can have either a straight edge for carving straight lines (left), or a curved edge for curved lines (right).

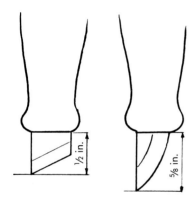

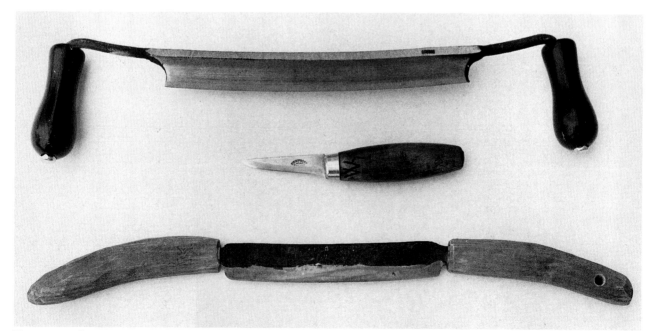

From top to bottom: a drawknife, a worn Mora knife and a hand-forged splitting knife.

country. The shaving horse is an ingenious holding device that ideally complements the drawknife. The drawing below shows one kind of shaving horse. You place the blank on the slanted ledge and clamp it beneath the head of the horse when you push on the treadle. The more you pull on the drawknife, the more pressure you exert on the treadle with your foot, thereby increasing the head's grip on the blank.

There are two schools, plus variations, in the use of the drawknife. The bevel-up method, with the flat side of the blade riding on the blank, is preferred by some craftsmen. Some who use this method dub, or slightly round, the edge on the flat side of the blade. This gives you better control over the depth of cut and allows you to come up out of the wood if the drawknife digs. This usually happens when the knife starts cutting into the grain.

Another method is to work with the bevel down, letting the bevel of the drawknife ride on the blank. I prefer this method because it gives me more control and makes it easier to work convex surfaces. I do flip the drawknife over when the work calls for it, such as on flat surfaces when I am certain that I will not start cutting into the grain. You will have to experiment to see what suits you best.

The Swedish splitting knife was used to do just that, split wood. It was used to do approximately the same tasks as the froe, riving and splitting out shakes and shingles. Splitting knives are seldom used for splitting today, but they are used by some craftsmen as cutting tools. The splitting knife is similar to the drawknife, except that it has a bevel on both sides of the blade and handles that usually extend straight out from the blade. Splitting knives found on the market today have very

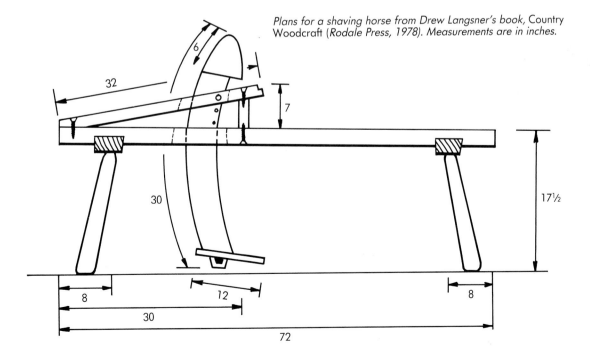

Plans for a shaving horse from Drew Langsner's book, Country Woodcraft *(Rodale Press, 1978). Measurements are in inches.*

short blades, only about 115mm (4½ in.) long. They are usable, but older ones made in the 1930s and 1940s had much longer blades, making them more effective when taking long strokes.

The straight handles on the splitting knife make the tool useful for bench work because they stay clear of the bench, and you can push the tool as well as pull. The handles will not give you the advantage of leverage that you have with the offset handles of the drawknife, so the splitting knife is harder to control.

Axes, Hatchets and Adzes

Early axes were often general-purpose tools used as weapons and striking tools, as well as for felling trees, clearing brush and shaping wood or stone. Many axes sold today are still general-purpose tools, used for everything from splitting kindling to pulling nails.

In a historical perspective, saws and sawmills are late developments. Axes were used to fell trees, hew round stock into timber and shape wood into implements and woodenware. To accomplish these tasks better, some axes developed into tools for specific purposes. Whereas both polled and double-bit felling axes fit their purpose well, they are not efficient for hewing. Heavy broad axes with long, wide blades remove more wood and leave a smooth surface several times larger than that possible with a felling ax. Small broad axes or hewing hatchets shape wood into implements and woodenware with great precision.

Hewing hatchets—Hewing hatchets and broad axes have much in common. They have thick bits above the edge to give them weight and balance. Their bevels are ground flat, with one bevel wide and the other narrow. The wide bevel registers and gets support from the surface cut by the edge. The narow bevel breaks away the waste. Right-handed axmen use hewing axes with the wide bevel on the left; the opposite is true for left-handed axmen.

Hewing hatchet bevels

If you're right handed, a long left bevel will give you more support when hewing. The total angle should be 24° to 30°, depending on the quality of the tool's steel and the hardness of the wood you are working.

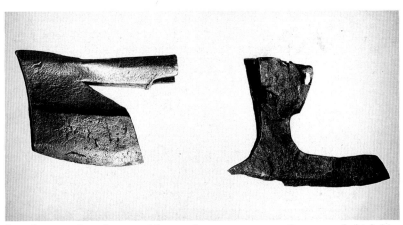

Scandinavian broad axes with tapering eyes, narrow throats and thick bits above the cutting edges.

The primary purpose of the hewing hatchet is to shape wood. The cutting edge on these hatchets can vary in length from slightly longer than the edge of a felling ax to the edge length of a smaller broad ax. Edge lengths of 12cm to 23cm (4¾ in. to 9 in.) are common. Most of these hatchets are hand forged with edges of forge-welded carbon steel sandwiched between mild steel. Because they are one-of-a-kind axes, they also vary in shape and weight.

Hewing hatchets have shorter handles than broad axes and felling axes. When you work with them, you usually choke up on the handle, making a long handle unnecessary. I have seen very heavy Norwegian hewing hatchets with handles no longer than 20cm (8 in.).

The hewing hatchet is often powered only from the wrist and forearm, the movement being that of a pendulum reinforced by the upper arm and shoulder. The combination of the hewing hatchet's long cutting edge, a long, wide bevel and the momentum gained through the weight of the head lets you hew with great precision. You can put a point on a match if you want to. Sometimes the hewing hatchet is used also as a knife, with the wrist locked and slicing with the blade at an angle. Shipwrights and carpenters often sharpen their pencils with the hewing hatchet, using only four strokes to complete the task.

Hewing hatchets have short handles because you usually choke up on the handle for fine work. The narrow throat lets you grasp the tool directly behind the edge.

On the other hand, when a skilled axman with a razor-sharp hewing hatchet grasps the handle far out, he has the capacity to waste away surprisingly large quantities of wood. There are few persons today who realize the versatility of the hewing hatchet. I am convinced that hewing also develops a sense for design in a way no industrial process or machine can do.

The hatchet—A hatchet is a small light ax with a short handle. It is easy to carry and is often used as a general-purpose tool. Usually only one hand is used to wield it. Most hatchets available today, when not specified as hewing hatchets, are factory-ground with rounded, convex bevels like those on larger felling axes. These hatchets can be reground with flat bevels, one wider than the other (see the drawing on p. 22), and used like hewing hatchets to shape wooden objects. Hatchets with very thin bits may have to be rounded slightly on the side of the narrow bevel so they will stand up to use.

The hewing hatchet is also capable of wasting large amounts of wood. The stroke begins above your head, and the long edge of the blade slices through the wood at an angle.

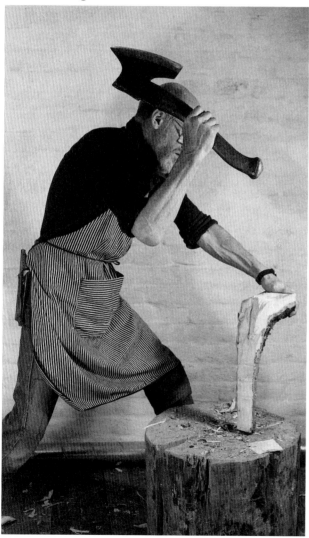

Ax handles—It is essential to consider the shape of the ax handle. On small hatchets, it is possible to make do with a standard manufactured handle, but standard handles often come with slippery lacquered finishes. Rough such a handle with a rasp before using it to give you a better grip.

You will probably not be able to find a standard handle that can be hung at the correct angle to the edge of a hewing hatchet—you want the edge to slice through the wood at an angle. In most cases, you will have to make the handle yourself. Choose wood that has high tensile strength, such as ash, hickory or oak. If you choose green wood, rough it out with an ax or a saw, and let it dry before fitting it to the eye. Avoid the pith (see p. 132). The grain should follow the shape of the handle you are making to avoid weak short grain. When the blank is dry, mount the head before doing the final shaping, so you can see and feel the hatchet as a whole.

The design is up to you, but be sure to keep the ax's function in mind. The handle should not be round, but rather egg shaped in section, with the narrower part on the belly of the handle in line with the edge. This is so you will be able to feel the direction of the edge. The handle's thickness should fit your own hand for a comfortable grip along the entire length of the handle. Usually it can be thicker at the eye where you will choke up on it for fine work. At the eye, the thumb and middle finger should at least touch each other. The index finger will be extended down the narrow-bevel side of the hatchet for control when doing fine work.

The handle can taper toward the butt to give you a secure grip when making high, powered strokes. The butt should be flared or have a knob, so it will not slip from your hand. When designing the flare or knob, it is important to have the end grain in line with the handle where you will strike the butt to pound the handle into the eye. On standard handles, a striking surface is sometimes rendered by cutting the tip off the butt. Once again, the handle should not be slippery smooth, but it should not give you splinters either. Treating the handle with boiled linseed oil is a good idea.

When you are satisfied with the fit, you should wedge the handle. Remove it from the eye and make a kerf cut no more than two-thirds the length of the eye with a saw. Most hatchets and Kent-type axes have wedges in line with the ax head. Some European types with small tapered top openings have wedges perpendicular to the edge. Make a wedge that is the length of the kerf and long enough to facilitate tapping it home.

Bevel the top edges of the wedge to prevent splitting. Handles often loosen in shops or houses during the heating season. Therefore, leave the wedge 6mm (¼ in.) or so proud of the handle's end grain so it can be tapped in when necessary to tighten the fit.

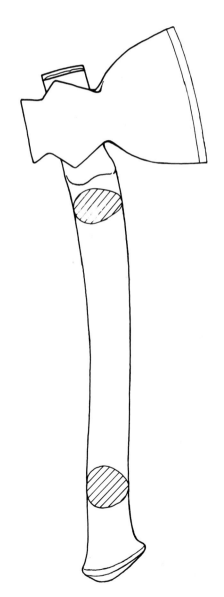

The hollowing adz—Axes with blades perpendicular to their handles have probably been in use as long as other axes. I have seen stone axes with hollowing bits. Axes of this kind, or adzes, are found almost everywhere in the world. In the northern part of Sweden, the hollowing adz fell into obscurity during the past half-century. In southern Sweden, it disappeared from use even earlier.

Hollowing adzes found in Sweden and Norway usually have their bevels on the outside. This outside bevel makes it possible to come up out of the wood, releasing the chip. Scandinavian adzes have been used mainly for hollowing troughs and bowls. Hollowing-adz heads vary in curve along their length, and have sweeps from very deep to almost flat. Adz heads with little curve along their length can be fitted with a long handle, such as the one shown in the photo below, and wielded with two hands like a polled ax. With an adz like this, however, it isn't possible to make a smooth transition from the wall to the bottom on small bowls, because of the lack of curvature in the adz head. To hollow small bowls, it is necessary to use a more curved adz. Adzes of this kind make it possible to use a pendulum stroke, with the wrist at the center.

An adz bevel should be flat. Bevel support on the blank is as important with the adz as it is with the knife and hewing hatchet. The bevel's angle and the handle's angle in relation to the head's curve along its length determine the radius of the adze's arc. The adz must be helved so the handle and the head function as a single unit. On short, one-handed adzes, the knob at the end of the handle is positioned in the palm of your hand. The power generated by the stroke must be transferred to the edge without sacrificing precision.

Adzes, used for hollowing, can be relatively straight with long handles, like the one pictured at top, whose overall length is 485mm (19 in.). But hollowing small bowls require curved, short-handled adzes. All three adzes were designed by the author and forged by Bengt Rönnqvist in Töre, Sweden.

Chopping blocks—Chopping blocks are found in all sizes, depending on their use, the user and the material available. Their height can range from 50cm to 70cm (20 in. to 27½ in.). Low blocks are fine when you want to sit on a stool to hew small objects. Blocks should be at least 22cm (9 in.) in diameter, preferably larger. The heavier and denser the wood, the better the block. If the block is full of knots, that's fine. The knots will help to subdue radial cracking and keep the block from splitting. A rough, uneven surface on the block will keep the blank from slipping. If you move a green-wood block indoors, make sure to stand it on a piece of plywood or other sheet material to keep moisture from ruining the floor.

It's an advantage to have blocks of different heights to accommodate blanks of different lengths. You should definitely have a separate block for splitting round stock and firewood. The block for hewing must be kept absolutely free from dust, dirt and sand. Otherwise, your razor-sharp ax will be nicked and dulled by abrasive particles on the block's surface. For some reason, your foot always seems to lift itself up on a chopping block when you are standing next to one. Excellent protection for your block is a piece of plywood with a few blocks nailed to the bottom to keep it in place.

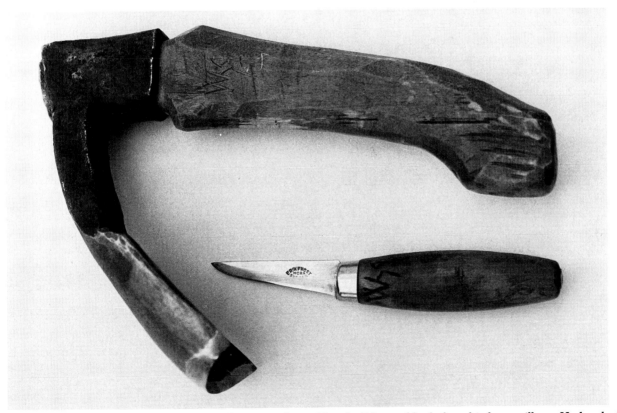

This is Sundqvist's best adz for hollowing large troughs and bowls. It's an old adz from his home village. He has had it resteeled, that is, a new carbon steel insert has been forge-welded to the mild steel back-up. From the edge to the poll it is 185mm (7¼ in.) and weighs 1.02kg (2¼ lb.).

Edge Protection

A cutting tool with a razor-sharp edge should be kept that way. Take pains to keep edge tools clear of other tools and objects that might dull or nick them. Be especially careful to keep them away from abrasives and abrasive dust. It's a good idea to put your carving tools away before starting to sand.

A knife sheath—Any tool that will be carried with you should have some kind of edge protection. If your knife lacks a sheath, here is a simple way to make one from birch bark:

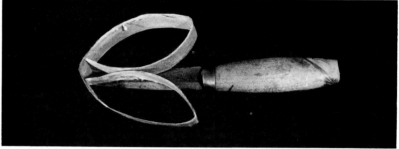

A. Cut a strip of birch bark slightly wider than the width of your knife blade. The strip should be four times as long as the blade, plus 2cm to 3cm (¾ in. to 1¼ in.). Fold the bark inward, with the cambium (brown) side facing outward.

B. Clamp the folded strip with a clothespin. Cut a narrower strip that will be long enough to be wrapped into a helix up the entire length of the sheath. The starting end should be trimmed at an angle to start the helix. Wind tightly.

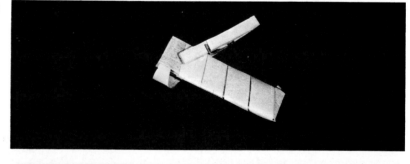

C. Finish by cutting the end of the strip at an angle, and tuck it under the folded inner bark. Pull it through and trim off the protruding end.

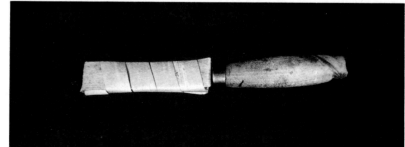

D. Your sheath is now ready for use. The nonslippery surface of the birch bark helps to keep the knife in place.

A sheath for carving hooks—Carving hooks are subject to more damage and dulling than knives, because they're often put aside with their edge down. Protection for the edges of these tools is almost as important as the tool itself. Here is an example of easy-to-make protection for a carving hook:

A. Cut a couple of strips of thin leather that will completely cover the sides of the hook's blade, above. An additional strip, 6mm to 8mm (¼ in. to ⁵⁄₁₆ in.) wide, will be needed as the insert strip in front of the edge. It's a good idea to have a piece of leather in front of the tip of the hook to protect it, too. This piece can be a long strip that can also be used to wrap around the sheath and hook. Use contact cement to glue the inner parts together. Follow the curve of the hook when you press the leather parts together, wrapping tightly with the long strip.

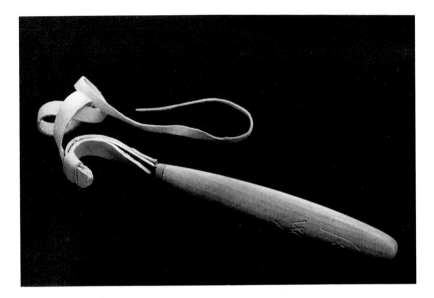

B. The finished sheath. Unwind the long leather strip to slide the hook from its channel.

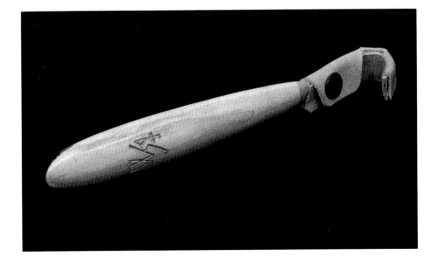

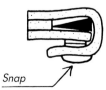

Snap

C. An alternative to wrapping the sheath with a strip is to make one of the leather sides of the sheath wider, making a flap on which a small snap can be mounted.

Ax and adz sheaths—Axes and adzes deserve sheaths, which can be sewn or riveted from leather. But a quick and equally effective sheath can be made from a short length of garden hose, slit and secured over the edge with heavy rubber bands.

A tool roll—The tool roll shown below is sewn with staggered pockets to facilitate safe storage of carving tools. A tool roll should be wide enough to keep the longest tools 7cm to 9cm (2¾ in. to 3½ in.) from the outer edge of the roll. A tie strap secures the roll.

Safety
Without a doubt, it is possible to cut yourself with a knife. When using knives, you must learn certain rules. When these rules have become habits, the risk of having an accident will be small. You will then be able to concentrate on the satisfaction and joy of working with a knife.

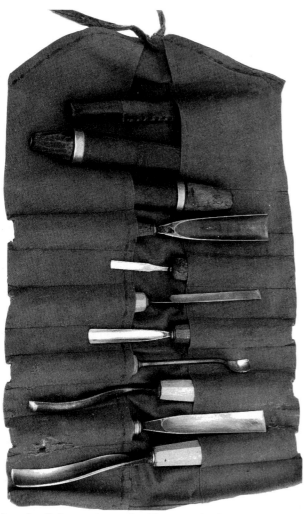

A tool roll for carving tools. Flaps on the long sides would add protection.

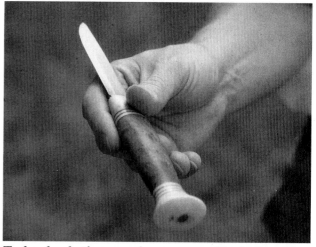

To hand a knife to another person safely, begin with a common grip. Flick the handle forward and rotate your hand. The handle is ready to take, with the back of the blade safely toward the web of your thumb.

Handing and receiving a knife—A long time ago, my brother and I were in the kitchen in our home, and somehow we both got the idea that we wanted to try mother's kitchen knife at the same time. My brother grabbed the handle, and I the blade. I still have scars on three of my fingers from that incident.

Almost everyone knows that you should hand a knife to someone by presenting the handle first. Even so, accidents happen when the receiver pulls it away without thinking and the person presenting the knife discovers his hand in the wrong place.

A safe way to present a knife to someone is to hold the knife edge down, as if you were going to slice vegetables on a cutting board. Then flick the handle forward, pivoting at the bolster between your thumb and index finger. If you rotate your wrist clockwise, the handle will be ideally positioned for an exchange. Even if the receiver wrenches it from your hand, the edge is safely away from you.

Unsheathing the knife—Accidents often happen when knives are being unsheathed. Mora-knife handles taper toward the blade; their sheaths follow the form of the handle and usually do not extend beyond the thickest part of the handle. This means the knife can be wedged into the sheath. The harder it is pushed into its sheath, the harder it is to unsheathe it. A knife that is stuck can be safely released by grasping the sheath with one hand and, without trying to jerk it out, twisting it back and forth until it releases.

Lappish knives and many other handmade knives have sheaths that lock onto the handle, because the leather extends past the thickest part of the handle and the opening resists the handle being withdrawn. It is important to remember that when you unsheathe the knife, the blade will suddenly release when the thickest part of the handle passes the narrow opening. This sudden release poses a danger for the uninitiated. The knife can cut through the sheath and into your hand, or the uncontrolled knife could injure someone else. Usually you remove the knife from the sheath with your carving hand. If the knife is not seated too tightly, you can release it with one hand by grasping the handle and pushing against the upper part of the sheath with your thumb. You can stabilize the sheath by grasping it with your opposite hand. If the knife is actually stuck, it's a good idea to put the thumb of this opposite hand on top of your knife hand, pushing and controlling the knife at the same time. It's also a good idea to let the back of the knife ride on the sheath when unsheathing and when returning the knife to its sheath. This will prevent cutting the sheath.

Control of movement and stance—You must use a certain amount of force to cut through wood with a knife, and when the knife leaves the wood, by will or by accident, it must be stopped to avoid injury to yourself or others. Each knife stroke, you will see, must have a control or stop.

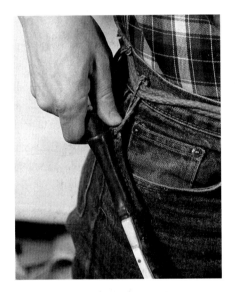

Use your thumb to help release a fully sheathed knife. For knives that are difficult to unsheathe, use the thumb of the opposite hand for reinforcement.

It is easiest to carve when sitting on a low stool or chair without armrests. This makes it easy for you to get the control you need for your forearms and elbows. Even when sitting in a chair, it is important to keep a safe distance from others. When carrying or working with knives or other edge tools, be aware that you have something that is potentially dangerous to yourself and others. Carry your knife with the tip down when you are close to other people, and don't talk with your hands if you have a knife in one of them. When you lay your knife aside, think about who might come in contact with it; it could be a child, for instance. Avoid accidents by anticipating their possibility.

Ax safety—During my days as a manual-arts teacher, I never had an an accident with an ax. But once I had a very close call with my son Ola. I decided to take him with me to the school shop, where I was going to rough out a large bowl.

In the shop, I gave him some toys about 10 feet away from the chopping block and put some boxes between us to protect him from the chips. I took my ax and started working on the bowl. Suddenly, in the middle of a stroke and with no chance of stopping it, I saw Ola's small fingers slip under the bowl. As if help came from Above, the ax stayed in the bowl and did not follow through into the block. I put my ax away and we went home.

You or someone else can be seriously injured if you work haphazardly with an ax. It is the momentum an ax gains from its weight that makes it work effectively, but it is also the momentum that can cause serious injury. It is therefore necessary to follow basic safety rules when working with an ax. From others and from my own experience, I have learned to take the following precautions:
—When you work with an ax, make certain there is plenty of distance between you and anyone close by.
—When you lay your ax aside, even for short periods, put it in a safe place where it won't be a hazard.
—Don't leave your ax lying on top of the chopping block with the handle sticking out. This is especially dangerous if the ax is a long-edged hewing hatchet. It could easily be knocked off the block and land on someone's toe.
—Driving the top corner of a hewing hatchet into your block may be a tempting way to store it, but the long, unprotected edge could easily cut you or someone else. Don't leave it that way.
—If you carry an ax any distance, the edge should be protected. Even over short distances, you must be aware of others close by, and of what could happen if you tripped and fell.
—If you lean an unprotected ax against a wall, make certain that you turn the edge toward the wall.
—You must be even more cautious if there are children nearby. They can make fast, unanticipated moves.

Sharpening

Grinding

If you are going to find enjoyment in working with cutting tools, it is of utmost importance that they be sharp. In many large shops, dull knives are not sharpened, but replaced by new ones. New knives as such are not suitable for carving.

New knives are often factory ground with very acute edge angles. In the case of the Mora knife, the edge angle is usually 19° to 20°. A few manufacturers grind their knives to even more acute angles. Knives with very acute edge angles are not able to withstand much use without chipping, and therefore must be rounded somewhat to support the edge. This is more or less what happens in the factory when the knives are ground and polished. The knife pictured below is a new knife, as it came from the manufacturer. The enlargement shows part of the blade with the bevel, and a narrow line at the very edge. This narrow line is the ever-so-slightly rounded edge reflecting light. A knife like this will work fine for hunting, fishing, cutting vegetables and strip-

A factory-new Mora knife. An enlargement of the bevel reveals the slightly rounded edge highlighted by the light reflecting from it.

ping electrical wires. It will even work for wasting large quantities of wood when roughing out blanks. But it will not work well when you want to shape objects and finish carve. For precise carving and detail work, you need to have exact control over the amount of wood being removed. This kind of carving requires that the bevel be flat and not rounded in the least.

When the edge is rounded (as shown in the drawing at left) and the bevel is placed flat on the blank, the edge will not touch the surface of the blank. To make the knife cut, you will have to raise the back of the knife. You will thus be riding on the short bevel formed by the rounded edge. This means that you will not be able to use the support of the bevel proper. It is the bevel proper that supports and controls the edge in the cut and determines how much or how little wood will be removed. Thus, knives with rounded edges, whether rounded in the manufacturing process or through improper grinding and honing, will have to be reground and honed to give them flat bevels.

The flat bevel—Flat bevels are imperative on carving knives and equally important on most other cutting tools, such as hewing hatchets, carving hooks, gouges and turning tools used for shearing. Many people with considerable experience with cutting tools do not understand or make use of this fundamental principle. The reason may be a lack of proper training, but to a large extent it seems to be a result of the increased use of machines on the job. Power can obscure the importance of a proper cutting edge.

High-speed grinders—In a pinch, a person with considerable experience with high-speed grinders may be able to grind a knife on them. One of the pitfalls of using such a grinder, even a large one, is the tendency to get an uneven or hilly bevel. This is because of the difficulty of gaining the support of your entire body and stance when grinding on a small diameter wheel. Beyond this, it is difficult to register or feel the bevel against the running surface of the hard wheel, and this makes it nearly impossible to maintain the same bevel angle along the entire length of the knife.

The next pitfall is that it's almost impossible to grind a knife on a high-speed grinder without burning the carbon steel. Because of the heat buildup caused by friction, the steel is annealed and becomes too soft for carving purposes. This becomes evident when the steel takes on a bluish hue. When this happens, care must be taken to grind away the annealed part of the blade. At worst, the knife may have to be retempered. Because of these problems, I recommend that carving knives and other cutting tools be ground on a wet grindstone.

Wet grinders—It's an advantage to grind knives on a large-diameter grindstone, such as 450mm to 600mm (18 in. to 24 in.). The larger the stone, the easier it is to grind knives without the help of supports or jigs. The grit should not be too fine, and the stone should

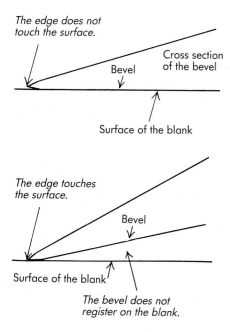

The edge does not touch the surface.

Bevel

Cross section of the bevel

Surface of the blank

The edge touches the surface.

Bevel

Surface of the blank

The bevel does not register on the blank.

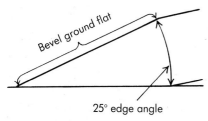

Bevel ground flat

25° edge angle

The edge and whole bevel are in contact with the blank.

not be too hard. Very hard or very fine stones will tire you by removing metal too slowly. Hard or fine stones also make it difficult to feel when you have the bevel flat on the running surface of the stone.

The Tormek grinder pictured below is a good one, in spite of the small 250mm (10-in.) stone. It is supplied with an excellent tool rest, a number of jigs and stone-dressing accessories. The jigs for chisels, plane irons and gouges all work very well. There are also a couple of jigs for knives with fine adjustment controls. A nice feature is that these jigs allow you to grind the opposite bevel by merely flipping the jig over without removing the knife. This works only on larger knives, however, and smaller knives will have to be removed to reverse sides. The smaller of the two jigs is suitable for sloyd and carving knives. The machine comes with or without a motor; the one without a motor hooks up to almost any electric drill.

The grinder also has a honing wheel to the right of the stone that runs at the same rpm as the stone. In my opinion, the honing wheel works well on general-purpose knives, but is not sufficient for the razor-sharp edge needed on a carving knife.

A knife-grinding jig on a Tormek wet grinder.

Tormek has recently marketed a new optional stone called Tormek Super Grind for its grinders. This stone removes steel faster than conventional natural stones. The Super Grind stone costs about three times as much as the standard stone, but it is supposed to last three times as long.

The Kiruna wet grinder, pictured on p. 46, comes in three different sizes. The smallest two, employing a 350mm (14-in.) and 275mm (11-in.) stone respectively, are planned to be marketed in the U.S. by General Electric in 1990. Kiruna grinders incorporate a smaller-diameter high-speed grinder for general grinding. Although the tool rests provided on these units are somewhat flimsy, they do work well when grinding chisels and plane irons; they are of no use when grinding knives. Knives must be ground freehand or supported by a grinding stick like the one illustrated on p. 43.

There is a Delta grinder now on the United States market that incorporates a 250mm (10-in.) wet wheel and a 125mm (5-in.) high-speed stone, but I have not had the opportunity to try it. There are also various older large-diameter wheels that can be hand-cranked or pulleyed to a motor for slow-speed wet grinding. These may require some jury rigging, but they will have advantages over a high-speed grinder.

One thing that I would like to see, but have not found on any of the grinders, is an effective splatter guard that does not get in the way of the operator. Another thing that I miss on almost all of the wet grinders is an adjustable water trough. When the stones are new and at

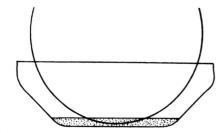

The water trough is too high; the stone carries sediment around on the grinding surface.

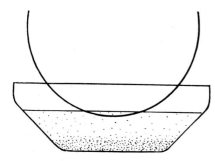

Sediment can sink to the bottom of the trough; the grinding surface remains clear.

An extension hook on a wet-grinder trough lowers the trough and keeps the stone from stirring up sediment.

their maximum diameter, they go all the way down into the sludge, and do not permit the residue to settle. Even if a large amount of water is used, the particles still follow with the water on the running surface of the stone. This makes it difficult, if not impossible, to see how the bevel of the knife is riding on the running surface of the stone. Besides that, the muddy water makes a mess. On some of the grinders it is possible to solve the problem by making a hook like the one pictured on the facing page to lower the trough.

Keeping the sandstone in trim—Sooner or later all sandstones become oval in shape because natural stones, which are not uniformly hard throughout, wear irregularly. Another cause of irregular wear is that the user at times forgets to lower or empty the trough after grinding. This will cause the lower part of the stone to swell because of water absorption. An oval stone or a deformed running surface makes it difficult to obtain satisfactory results.

Truing a stone is a simple matter. Ordinary galvanized water pipe 12mm to 30mm (½ in. to 1½ in.) in diameter, and not less than 400mm (16 in.) in length, is the tool for the job. You'll need a rest for the end of the pipe, and a board clamped to the frame of the machine will do fine. Hold the pipe in both hands, raise the butt end slightly and nudge the end of the pipe into the stone. Roll the pipe across the rest from the outside edges of the stone in toward the middle to avoid chipping the stone's edges. The photo below shows the correct position. Take small bites. Hold the business end of the pipe down firmly on the rest so that it won't ride on the stone and follow its oval shape.

You can true a sandstone into round by using a length of pipe supported on a clamped board.

A high-speed grinder helps to keep the pipe sharp. When the stone is round, remove the ridges by lowering the angle of the pipe to a straight-away position. Roll the pipe on the rest as before.

You can true up a stone either wet or dry. In either case you will turn up dust, so it's a good idea to wear a dust mask or a respirator. If you have a dust or smoke hood connected to a shop vac or dust-collection system, use it to keep the air clean.

The water trough should be emptied and cleaned now and then. Don't forget to lubricate the bearings, and if you own a model with a high-speed grinder on the side, check the oil level in the gear box.

Remove ridges from the stone by rolling the pipe flat on the rest across the running surface of the stone.

A high-speed grinder is used to sharpen the pipe.

Freehand grinding—When I speak of hand grinding, I don't mean that your hands alone are doing the work. Performing tasks by hand almost always entails coordinating other muscles and positioning your entire body in an appropriate stance. Muscular co-ordination and stance give you whole-body support when you are grinding, carving or doing other manual work.

You may feel that it's unnecessary to learn hand grinding, since I've already mentioned jigs that can do the work. But jigs are not univer-sally available or applicable. I believe that learning to grind your knife without the help of a jig is a step on the way to becoming a good carver and craftsman. Once you have mastered the art of grinding, you will be able to touch up your knife in seconds when it becomes difficult to hone it to a razor-sharp condition. Hand grinding will then be much faster than setting up and adjusting a jig. It will also develop the skill you need to grind other edge tools.

I also feel that hand grinding is an important part of our cultural heritage that should not be lost. For generations the craftsman has ground his tools on a revolving sandstone. Why shouldn't we give to posterity that which has been a gift from earlier generations? I believe there should be as much honor and satisfaction in being able to grind knives and carve as there is in being able to drive a car well, ski down-hill or participate in sports of any kind. Grinding by hand is an excit-ing and fascinating experience. You must first know what to do; the rest is practice.

Stone rotation—Whether the stone should rotate toward you or away from you when grinding edge tools has been a long-discussed question. I was brought up in the stone-toward-you school. This method gives me a better grip on the knife and also lets me gain better support from my stance. Those who advocate the stone-toward-you method usually point out that it results in a shorter burr. I'm not certain if it makes any difference whether the burr is long or short, as long as the edge angle remains the same. Certainly the quality of the steel will not be altered in either case. One thing that can happen when the stone is rotating toward you is that the edge can accidentally dig into the stone. Grinding with the stone rotating away from you will eliminate that problem. You will, however, not be able to exert as much pressure on the knife, and thus it will take more time to grind it.

Edge angles and bevels—Correct edge angles and bevels are important. What is the correct edge angle? As in the case of other edge tools used for cutting, there is a relationship between the hard-ness of the material you are working with and the quality of the steel in the knife. Harder wood requires a less acute edge angle. A knife will cut better if it has a more acute edge angle, but only so long as the steel will stand up to the use it is getting. If the steel is too hard for the angle given it, it will chip easily. If it is too soft for a given angle, it will dull quickly. In some cases the proper angle is a matter of the way you carve and how much force you use. The edge angles on my knives range between 22° and 26°.

The main difficulty in grinding a knife is obtaining an even bevel without ridges or facets, all the way from the handle to the tip of the blade. Minor ridges toward the back of the blade won't make much difference, but close to the cutting edge the bevel must be even. If there are nicks on the edge, they should be ground out by taking an equal amount of steel from each side of the blade. This will ensure that the edge is in the middle of the blade. In the case of laminated knives with a thin layer of carbon steel sandwiched between soft steel, it is essential that the cutting edge ends up where you have carbon steel. You should also try to get both bevels as close to the same width as possible. The slight hollow grind you get on the bevel when using a large-diameter stone is no problem. In fact it probably serves as proof that the bevel is not convex. A slightly concave bevel can be honed many times without becoming convex.

Practice on knives that you are not afraid to lose. It doesn't take long to grind up a few knives when practicing. On your favorite knives, try not to grind up to the very edge, unless they are nicked or very dull. The little bit of the old edge left on the blade can be honed away, and you will save steel and make the knife last longer.

Grinding grips—Now we will get down to the business of actual grinding. I'm going to show you a couple of grips that I have found to work best for me. Naturally, you should experiment to find the grips that suit you.

To grip the knife for grinding, hold the handle in your fingers and place your thumb at the back of the blade.

In grinding, the fingers of one hand support the blade toward its back, while the thumb of the same hand rests on the knuckle of the hand holding the knife.

Study the photos below and those on the facing page. Notice how the handle of the knife is held with the fingers, and that support is given to the back of the blade or the handle with the thumb. Gripping the knife in such a manner will give you a better chance to feel when you have the bevel of the knife flat on the running surface of the grinding stone.

If the blade of the knife is long enough, place all of the fingers of your opposite hand along the back of the knife, and rest the thumb of that hand on the knuckle of the thumb on the hand holding the knife for support. At this point you should feel as if your hands are supporting each other, which should make you feel more secure. To gain even more support along the back of the knife, I usually let my elbow rest against my hipbone.

Stance is very important, as it lends the support necessary to make the body into one solid unit. Your stance should be wide, with the foot on the handle side placed well forward alongside the grinder and the other foot placed directly behind the running surface of the stone (as shown in the photo at right).

When you feel you have the correct grip, relax your hands, place the back edge of the bevel lightly on the stone and tip the knife forward until the bevel is riding on the running surface of the stone. You should be able to see that the water flow is slowed down when the back edge of the bevel starts resting on the stone, and that the speed of the water flow increases as you tip the edge of the blade toward the stone. You will feel when the wheel finds the bevel. If you tip the edge too far and lift the back of the bevel from the stone, you will grind an

Whole-body support is essential to knife grinding. The stance is wide, with the foot opposite the knife hand positioned far back.

When the bevel is flat on the stone, water flows freely over the blade.

Grinding the blade's tip. The handle is raised and pulled slightly backward, following the curve of the blade.

undesirable edge angle or get a double bevel. This is something you cannot see, but you will feel less resistance, and so it is important to keep your hands as relaxed as possible.

When you are certain that you have the knife in the right position, lock your upper arms and shoulders, then use moderate downward pressure on the knife and move it slowly back and forth across the running surface of the stone. When you get to the rounded tip of the knife, try to maintain the same angle while raising the handle of the knife so that it will be ground all the way to the tip. From the tip you should grind all the way back to the handle in one pass. The knife pictured on p. 41 appears to have a shorter bevel toward the tip, but this is because it has a hand-forged blade whose thickness tapers toward the tip.

Knives and other cutting tools that have bevels on both sides of the blade are usually ground completely on one side first, then reversed and ground on the other side. This means that the grip will be the same, but you will have to switch hands and change your stance to the opposite of what it was for the first side of the blade.

The burr, or wire edge, will appear when the second bevel is ground to where it meets the first bevel. If you move your finger tips from the back of the bevel across the edge, you will feel the burr. When you are satisfied that you have met the edge of the first bevel, make an additional swift and light stroke from the tip of the knife to the handle, or from the handle to the tip. Switch back to the first-ground bevel and

The back of the bevel is placed lightly on the running surface of the stone (A), then the edge is tipped forward until it rides flat on the stone (B).

A

B

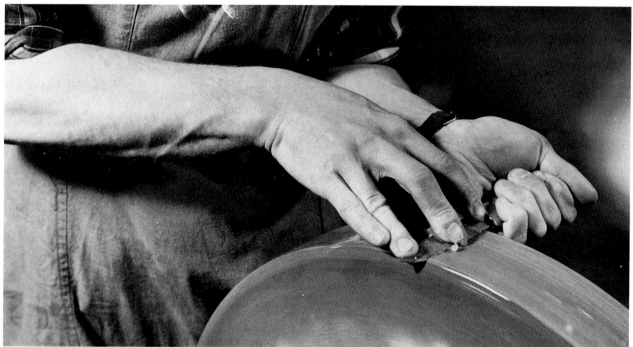

When a palm-up grip is used, the elbows gain support from the sides of the body and the hips.

make a final light stroke there also. These light strokes make the striations on the bevels shallower, making honing faster.

An alternative grip is shown in the photo on the facing page. The hand grips the knife palm up, instead of palm down. This grip positions your knife-hand's arm back far enough so that the elbow can rest against your hipbone. This gives you solid support for both elbows, but it seems to lessen the amount of sensitivity in the hand and increase the difficulty of finding and maintaining the correct bevel angle. Notice also that the fingers are held slightly closer to the bevel to enable you to exert more pressure on the blade. This compensates for the decreased downward pressure you are able to exert when gripping the knife handle with the palm up.

The grinding stick—A simple grinding stick will enable you to get a good hold on the knife and increase the amount of pressure on it. This is especially important when you are trying to waste away steel on a damaged or nicked knife, or if you are going to change the edge angle.

The grinding stick should be made of a wood that has a fair amount of tensile strength, such as birch, mountain ash or maple. The back of the knife blade should fit firmly in the mouth of the stick, as shown in the drawing at right. The lower lip should not be thick, but beveled so it does not ride right on the stone. A lower lip will not be possible on sticks used with very small knives, and in this case the stick will touch the grindstone.

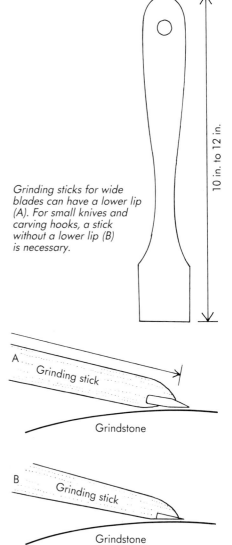

Grinding sticks for wide blades can have a lower lip (A). For small knives and carving hooks, a stick without a lower lip (B) is necessary.

Grinding with the aid of a grinding stick.

I'm surprised that such a simple device hasn't been used more often. It's not a jig, because it does not give fixed support in relation to the running surface of the stone. A grinding stick requires much practice to master, and I would suggest that finish grinding on knives be done without it. It can be especially helpful, however, especially when hand grinding tools that are difficult to hold and move, like spokeshave irons and carving hooks.

Grinding gouges—Grinding a gouge is actually much easier than grinding a knife. This is because the entire tool and the handle are directly in back of the edge. And because gouges have considerable length, it's easy to get a good grip on them.

As with grinding knives, the stance is wide, with one foot as far back as possible. If you're holding the handle with your right hand, your right foot should be placed in the back position, and vice versa if the handle is in your left hand. The arm of the hand holding the handle should be pressed tightly against your body or braced against your chest. Rest the finger tips of the opposite hand on the edge of the flute, and roll the bevel back and forth across the running surface of the stone. Make certain that the bevel remains straight and even, without ridges and facets. After grinding gouges and gouge-like tools, there will be ridges and unevenness on the surface of the stone, so it's a good idea to refinish the surface of the stone as described earlier.

The gouge is moved back and forth across the stone's running surface at the same time it is rolled from side to side over the entire bevel.

Grinding carving hooks—Grinding a carving hook is essentially the same as grinding a gouge, except that the handle is in line with the working edge, like a knife, instead of in back of it. This means that it is hard to get support in back of the blade, but using a grinding stick will solve the problem. If you hold the handle in your left hand and the stick in your right, the right foot should be placed as far back as possible.

A grinding stick adds support and control when grinding a carving hook. Move the tool as you would a gouge.

Grinding axes—Grinding an ax is not too different from grinding a knife, except that you have much more to hold on to. Here are three grips that can be used to grind an ax:

A. Hold the ax handle from below with one hand, palm up, as close to the head as possible. The thumb of your other hand can be in back of the poll, with your fingers pressing on the blade close to the edge. Support your elbows on your hips and lock your upper arms against your sides. In this instance, your stance should be wide, with the foot opposite the hand that is on the handle close to the grinder and the other foot far back.

B. Grasp the ax handle with your palm down, the thumb and two or three fingers on the blade, depending on how wide it is. Your index finger and maybe the middle finger of that hand should also exert pressure on the blade close to the edge. Your other hand adds more pressure. As with the other grips, lock your arms against your sides, support your elbows on your hips and position the leg opposite the hand holding the handle back.

C. If it is necessary to remove a lot of steel, you can use a piece of lath or dowel to increase pressure on the ax head. Your right hand clasps the dowel and the handle at the same time as your elbow gains support from the hip. The poll is in the web of the elbow of your left arm; your left hand grasps the opposite end of the dowel. When your left hand presses down on the dowel, it levers the edge toward the stone, while your right leg, in its far-back position, counteracts the push of the rotating stone. Notice that this stance is the reverse of those mentioned earlier.

In all these grips, you can keep the edge at an angle to the sides of the stone to reduce the amount of concavity in the bevel. This is especially important when grinding on small-diameter stones, because the bevel would otherwise become too concave, weakening the edge.

Ax edges are usually curved, and it is important to keep moving the edge back and forth following that curve. Keep the bevel the same width along the entire edge. When the edge is at an angle, it should not be run out too far toward the bottom corner. That might bring the corner of the stone and the edge of the ax into a nasty encounter that would damage both stone and ax. You can go toward the top edge as far as you want without worry.

A hollowing adz is ground the same way as a gouge, except that the grip has to accommodate the angled handle.

A well-ground bevel, with the wire edge ready to be removed by honing.

Grinding hollowing adzes — Grinding an adz is the same as grinding a gouge, except that the adz doesn't have a handle straight out from the edge. Let the poll of the adz rest in the palm of your hand, grasping the lower part of the handle in the web of your thumb, as in the photo at left.

Honing
The grinder leaves behind rather deep scratches on the surface of the bevel. The edge becomes sawtoothed, and a burr or wire edge is formed. To get the edge sharp it must be honed, ridding it of the scratches and the burr. I prefer to do this by hand with sharpening stones. Honing with flat stones is the easiest way to maintain flat bevels on your knife.

Sharpening stones — You will need at least two, preferably three, stones. A good combination would be one coarse, fast-cutting stone, one medium stone and one fine finishing stone. There is a large assortment of reversible bench stones on the market. These are two stones laminated together, one coarse, the other fine. They include Carborundum with silicone carbide, coarse India with soft Arkansas and coarse India with fine India. Reversible stones do not have rounded edges, and thus cannot be used for honing gouge flutes.

Wedge-shaped slipstones with rounded edges are invaluable. These stones give you two flats for honing bevels and two different-sized rounds for gouge flutes. They are usually found in medium to fine grits. Readily available are a number of aluminum oxide, silicone carbide and Arkansas stones.

If you want a fine stone of the highest quality, I would suggest an Arkansas stone. These are without a doubt the finest stones available. They are quarried near Hot Springs, Arkansas, and are graded in increasing hardness and quality as follows: Washita, soft Arkansas, white hard Arkansas, and black hard Arkansas. The black stones were formerly used to hone straight-edged razors.

It's a good idea to mount your stones in a wooden base so that they can be held in a vise or otherwise clamped securely. Slipstones can be mounted so they give you a level surface to work on when you are honing knives, chisels, plane irons and other tools with straight edges.

Honing fluids — The surface of the sharpening stone consists of a multitude of abrasive particles with spaces between them. When you hone, small particles are abraded from the tool, and bits of the abrasive break from the stone. If you do not use a honing fluid, these metal particles and bits of stone will clog and glaze the stone's surface. Once the stone becomes glazed, it loses its effectiveness.

Thin oil, such as sewing-machine oil or commercial honing oil, are suitable for use on Carborundum, silicone carbide, India and Arkansas stones. In a pinch, you can thin a heavier oil with paint thinner or kerosene. Kerosene alone works well on fine, hard stones. On very hard, less porous stones, heavy oils seem to float the bevel above the abrasive particles on the surface.

If you use sandstones or clay stones, water should be used as the honing fluid. Water can even be used on oilstones like the ones mentioned above, but use a lot. Oil does a better job of lifting particles off the surface of the oilstone. Besides that, an oily edge cuts better than a dry edge, and it is also protected against rust.

Care of sharpening stones — Always keep the stones clean. Wipe them often, and don't wipe them with a cloth used to wipe a coarser stone or a knife honed on a coarser stone. Have a can of your honing fluid nearby so you can clean your stones occasionally.

It's a good idea to keep stones out of the dust by keeping them in a can or in their own covered box. They can be kept together with a plastic sponge drenched in oil, making them always ready for use. Just push the stone into the sponge and you are ready to go. When I'm traveling, I keep my stones in an old-fashioned metal pen box. I use cotton instead of a sponge in this box because it absorbs more oil.

Honing alternately on different parts of the stone's surface will wear the stone evenly. Hone toward the edges of the stone, right and left, not only in the middle. It's not easy to hone flat bevels and straight edges on an uneven stone.

Section of a wooden case made to fit an Arkansas slipstone. The mortise in the case keeps the stone level so it can be used for bench honing.

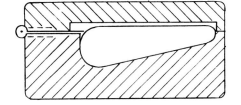

An old pen box with a bed of oil-drenched cotton houses sharpening stones: a white hard Arkansas (left), a medium Carborundum (upper right) and a black hard Arkansas (lower right).

Eventually stones will become uneven from wear. To true them, lap them on a flat piece of glass, using silicone carbide valve-grinding compound or silicone carbide grit (80 grit is good) as the abrasives. Valve-grinding compounds can be readily found at automotive-supply stores, and dry grits can be found at stores selling lapidary supplies, such as Grieger's (see Sources of Supply, p. 135). If you are using a water-based compound, thin it with water; if it is oil based, use kerosene or paint thinner. Dry grits should be mixed with water until you have a thin slurry. Lap the stone, using a circular movement, keeping an even, moderate pressure on it. Check the stone occasionally. You should be able to see low spots on the surface of the stone where the slurry builds up. Continue to lap until the low spots have completely disappeared. It's not a good idea to lap many stones on the same piece

The basic grip for honing knives: the index finger is placed so it can press the bevel flat on the stone.

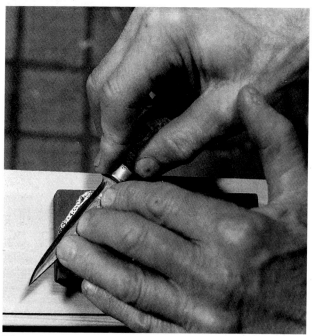

Three fingers of the opposite hand rest close to the back of the blade, while the thumb is placed on the knife-hand's thumb knuckle.

The honing stance is wide. Concentrate on keeping the bevel flat on the stone.

of glass, because low spots will eventually be lapped into the glass itself. Lapping on glass with low spots will create convex surfaces on your stones.

Honing a knife — Fix a mounted coarse stone in your workbench vise or clamp it to a worktable. Assume a wide stance that is approximately parallel to the length of the stone. Start honing your knife on the bevel you ground last. This will remove the burr faster in the honing process. I'll begin with the left bevel, and describe the correct grip for a right-handed person. A left-handed person would reverse this grip.

Look at the photo on the facing page and position the knife along the fingertips of your right hand, with your index finger at the hilt in line with the bevel. Grip the knife between your thumb and fingers so that it angles outward. The thumb should be against the back of the handle, and the index finger should be able to exert downward pressure on the bevel. The three long fingers of your left hand rest on the blade, giving it support. As in the case of grinding a knife, the thumb of the left hand should rest on the thumb knuckle of the right hand.

Rest the back of the bevel on the stone first, relax your grip and apply pressure with your right index finger until you feel the bevel resting flat on the stone. It is often recommended that a circular movement be used when honing, but I feel that it is easier to keep the bevel flat on the stone by rubbing back and forth in a straight line.

When you reach the curved bevel at the tip of the knife, you have to follow the bevel, keeping it flat on the stone and raising the handle slightly, and at the same time moving it inward toward the stone. This should result in a round, sweeping action. It will be difficult to feel the bevel on the stone at the very point of the knife because it is so narrow. By following through on the stroke, you will hone the same edge angle all the way to the point.

Examine the bevel occasionally and you will be able to see where you have been removing scratches caused by grinding. If the knife was ground concave, do not hone away the visible scratches in the middle of the bevel. The important thing is getting the edge sharp while the back of the bevel rests on the stone. In other words, don't hone more than necessary.

When you are satisfied with the first bevel, switch to the other one, keeping your fingers in approximately the same position. Place your thumb on this bevel where the index finger was on the first bevel. You can also position your thumb a little higher, just above the bevel. Experiment to find what fits you best.

On the opposite bevel, the thumb replaces the index finger to keep the bevel flat on the stone. The left thumb still braces the hands.

If you don't have a way to clamp the stone to your workbench, you can hold it down with one hand, and use the same grip on the knife handle as described above. You can also hold the stone in one hand, as shown in the photo below, left. Here you can choose between moving the knife over the stone and rubbing the stone against the bevel. Because you are holding the blade of the knife upward, you can see if the bevel is flat on the stone but it is still important to feel the bevel on the stone.

When you are satisfied that you have reached the edge with the coarse stone, it is time to switch to a finer stone. At this point you have two things to contend with: removing the scratches left by the coarse stone and honing away the burr. You can see the scratches left by the coarse stone in the photo below. The wire edge can be seen if you hold the knife close to a bright light, or better yet, look at it through a magnifying glass. You can also feel it by sliding your finger or fingernail over (not along) the edge.

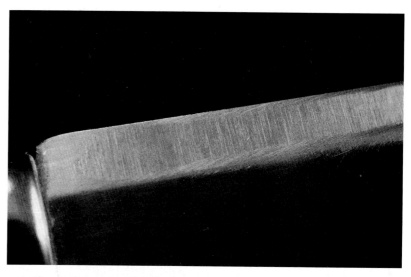

A circular motion is best when honing a knife on an unmounted stone. You can move the stone or the knife, whichever is more comfortable for you.

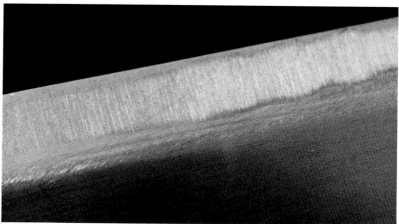

After honing with a coarse stone (top), the edge and back of the bevel have diagonal scratches. After honing with a black Arkansas stone (bottom), perpendicular striations from the grindstone are still visible, but the edge and back of the bevel are polished.

The procedure with the fine stone is the same as described earlier, except that you should switch bevels often to rid the edge of the burr as soon as possible. Do not be tempted to pull the burr off, because this would leave an undesirable jagged edge. This jagged or toothed edge could have microscopic flats that would require excessive honing to get the edge razor sharp. When the burr is gone, the knife should be sharp. You can see the shiny, polished edge and back of the bevel left by the Arkansas stone in the photo on the facing page.

Stropping—You can get your knife extra sharp by stropping it on a belt or strip of leather, preferably one glued to a flat board with contact cement. With the edge away from you and the bevel flat on the strop, pull the knife briskly toward you. Reverse direction by rolling the knife over the back of its blade, and make the next stroke away from you. Changing directions by rolling the knife on its edge tends to round and dull the edge. Continue stropping until you are satisfied that you have an extra keen edge. For faster results, you can rub buffing compound, found at almost any hardware store, into the strop.

Honing gouges—Begin by honing the bevel with your coarse stone. Hold the stone near the corner, supporting it along the side of the index finger. Hold the gouge upright and turn the bevel toward the stone so you'll be able to see and feel the bevel against the stone. Register the stone on the back of the bevel, then tip the stone,

Strop on a piece of leather glued to a flat board. Draw the knife away from the edge. To strop the other bevel, roll the knife over the back of the blade, not the edge.

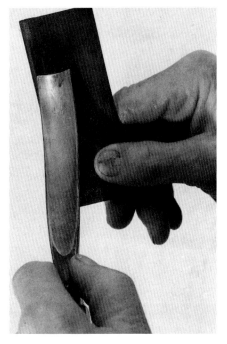

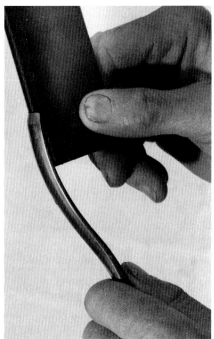

When honing the bevel of a gouge (top), learn to see and feel that the stone is flat on the bevel. The flute is the reference surface when honing the inside of a gouge (above). On bent gouges, very little of the flute should be used as a reference surface.

or the gouge, until you are firmly bridging the gap of the concave bevel (see the photo at left). Resist the temptation to lift the tool onto the edge. Move the stone up and down against the bevel, turning the entire tool back and forth as you proceed. Check now and then to make certain that you are keeping the bevel flat against the stone.

The flute of the gouge is honed next, using the round edge of a finer slipstone. It is unnecessary to use a coarse stone on the flute. Whether you start with a medium or fine stone depends on how well the flute is polished. Sit on a stool or chair without armrests, support your forearms on your knees, and press your upper arms against your sides. When honing straight gouges, keep the edge of the stone flat against the flute and stroke up and down along the length of the gouge. Make certain that you do not raise the stone from the flute, because this will round the inside edge of the tool. Once that edge becomes round, you will have to continue lifting the stone in order to hone it, changing the cutting angle. When you graduate to your fine finishing stone, alternate between bevel and flute frequently until the burr is gone.

Flutes on bent gouges should be honed by pressing only a small part of the length of the slipstone against the flute as close to the edge as possible. Use very short rubbing strokes to avoid registering the stone farther down along the curved flute, which would lift the stone and round the edge.

Honing carving hooks—Commercially offered carving hooks are not easy to hone. Basically, they should be honed as you would other gouges, but there is no flute to register on and the inside surface is seldom flat. The Frost hooks also have a short double bevel on the outside that develops when they are bending them at the factory. Grinding a flater bevel leaves too little steel, and thus, the edge

A motorized strop: the wooden axle with leather-covered wheels is mounted between lathe centers. One wheel is loaded with coarse buffing compound, the other with fine compound.

will not be of much use. Frost's Knivfabrik AB is presently trying to solve this problem, but for the moment, it will be necessary to make the best of the hooks available.

I would suggest honing the inside, slightly rounded surface by tipping the slipstone to where it meets the edge. Hone in a back-and-forth and slightly sliding action along the entire length of the blade, on both edges (the Frost hooks are double edged). The very short bevel on the outside will have to be used, but if it is rounded, I would grind out the roundness first. Then hone, trying to keep the stone as flat as possible on the short bevel.

Honing axes and adzes—Axes and adzes are no more difficult to hone than knives or gouges. As with the other tools, is is important not to round the edge.

Axes can be honed on a bench stone, using the palm-down grip you use when grinding them (see p. 46). Support the bevel with your index finger and the fingers of your other hand and rub it on the stone. Perhaps an easier way is to sit on a low bench with the ax between your legs. Rest the poll on the bench. Hone one bevel with the handle under your arm, the other with the handle away from you. Keep the stone flat on the bevel, rubbing the stone in circles. This method permits you to see and feel the stone on the bevel.

Adzes can be honed sitting down, with the poll resting between your legs. Otherwise, treat adzes as you would gouges.

Machine polishing and stropping—In most schools in Sweden today, honing is accomplished by buffing. Even if you grind a good bevel on an edge tool, a buffer will round it, and you'll sacrifice control in carving. On the other hand, if you are very careful when grinding and honing you can go one step further with the use of a motorized strop.

To make your own motorized strop, attach a wooden wheel to an axle, mount the axle between centers on a lathe and turn the wheel round. Take a piece of leather long enough to overlap on the circumference of the wheel and scarf the ends where they overlap, as with sanding belts, so the top seam will be away from the direction of travel on the wheel. Glue the strip to the wheel with contact cement, with the grain side toward the wheel. You can also have two wheels on one axle, as shown in the photo on the facing page, one loaded with a coarser buffing compound than the other.

Tools should be honed with the wheel turning *away* from the edge, not into it as with high-speed grinders. Ease the flat of the bevel onto the turning wheel and keep it flat on the wheel, moving the tool back and forth across its bevel. Use very light pressure and the slowest speed you have on your lathe to prevent heat buildup. Hone until you have a razor-sharp edge.

Ax
Work

Hewing with an Ax

To shape an object with an ax, it is necessary to use a technique other than one you would use when felling or limbing trees. When you hew on a chopping block, you do not chop the wood, you shear it. The cut starts at the near corner of the edge of the blade and slices toward the edge's far corner. This stroke, combined with the momentum gained through the weight of the ax, will let you cut with the entire length of the ax's edge. This technique also applies to axes with short edges, but precision is increased with long-edged axes because the bevel registers on more surface of the blank.

Because of this shearing action, your stance must be proper. Keep your feet wide apart. If you hew with your right hand, your right leg should be far back. This stance keeps your leg out of the path of the ax and also helps you gain power for your stroke. The ax head should be angled upward, with the hand well below it when making the stroke. It's a good idea to support the blank on the far side of the block, especially on powered strokes. If you miss or strike a glancing blow, you want the edge to end up in the block, not in your leg.

Start hewing low on the blank and work upward, but not to the top. Turn the blank upside down to work the opposite end. Work carefully in controlled increments. Don't take that last stroke after you've decided you're getting tired and should stop for a rest.

A safe stance while hewing has the legs wide apart and the blank well forward on the chopping block. This way, if the hatchet slips from the wood, it ends up in the block, not in your leg.

Make a Dough Bowl

Deformities in trees, such as burls, can be hollowed to make natural bowls or scoops. Traditional Swedish drinking vessels were made from burls, sometimes leaving part of the tree's trunk on the vessel to serve as a handle. The handle often had the shape of a goose's neck and head, hence their name, *ölgås* (beer goose). Larger troughs or bowls, however, are often made from split round stock. Feeding troughs, several feet in length, were made for livestock. Smaller troughs were used for making cheese, kneading bread and serving food.

Design—A bowl made from wood should be designed to be functional. Dough bowls need wide, long bottoms to keep them from tipping, and bowls for serving need handles. Basic Scandinavian bowl design is usually worked out from the rectangle of a split bowl blank, as seen in the plan views below. The bowls are usually at least twice as long as they are wide, and their walls are not very steep. This is especially important for the end-grain walls, which should be thicker than long-grain walls to ensure adequate strength. Handles can be included by extending the length of the bowl and undercutting for a finger hold. A common bowl shape is to curve the corners. If your blank is tapered, a boat-shaped bowl can be the attractive result. Bowls can also be taken from a split round with the pith side down. Such bowls will be shallow, but they will be graphically striking because the annual rings will follow the inner shape of the bowl.

Design variations for a doughbowl

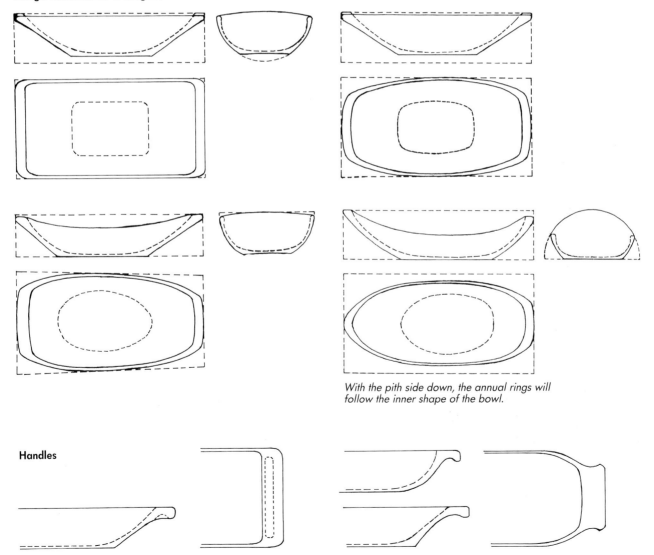

With the pith side down, the annual rings will follow the inner shape of the bowl.

Handles

Tools—You will need an ax or hewing hatchet, a hollowing adz and a couple of gouges to rough out the bowl. To true surfaces and do the finish carving, a knife, a drawknife or splitting knife, a spokeshave and a plane will be helpful. A stable workbench or a low bench with some means of securing the stock is an advantage. And of course, you will need a chopping block.

The size and sweep of the gouges (see p. 19) will depend on the technique used to work with them. Wide gouges will remove more wood, but they require more power. A gouge with a deep sweep is good for roughing out; a shallow gouge removes the ridges left by the deep gouge. A bent gouge is sometimes necessary to get in to smooth the bottom of the bowl.

Materials—Traditionally, softer woods have been used for troughs and bowls. Aspen and birch are among the first choices, but pine and spruce are not uncommon. Almost any kind of wood can be used, except for woods that are toxic, contain resins or in any other way might taint food. Alder, tulip poplar and basswood are easy to work. Maple, beech, mountain ash, juniper and fruitwood are a challenge, but the result is often a bowl you can be proud of.

Avoid wood with knots and uneven grain. The pith and some wood close to it should be removed to forestall radial checking. Whether you work with green wood or dry wood is often a question of what you have access to. Roughing out green wood is easy, but you must take measures to prevent checking and cracking when it dries (see pp. 132). If you are using green wood, leave the blank 10mm to 30mm (⅜ in. to 1⅛ in.) larger than you intend the final shape to be. This will permit you to make adjustments after the wood has dried.

Roughing out the blank—Choose a piece of round stock at least 4 in. longer than the bowl you want so you can trim off any checks that may develop. Remove the bark, split it down the middle and hew away the pith. Hew a flat on the opposite side and true the surface with a plane. This flat will become the bottom of the bowl.

Lay out the shape of the inner rim of the bowl on the blank, leaving about a 1-in. margin along the sides and perhaps twice that at the ends. The margin can vary depending on the strength of the wood you are using and the shape you are aiming for, but the end walls must be thicker than the side walls to accommodate the weaker short grain. If the ends will be shaped with handles, you will want to leave room for them, too. You can draw the shape freehand or make a symmetrical pattern by folding a piece of paper and drawing half the shape on the fold. Cut out the pattern with the paper still folded.

Use a hollowing adz with a short handle to hollow the bowl. The blank can be held at an angle on a chopping block or secured between the dogs of a cabinetmaker's workbench. But to get a longer, more powerful swing, a low bench fit with pegs and wedges, as shown in the

Hew the surface that will become the bowl bottom.

photo below, right, is ideal. You can straddle the bench, or stand to the side to work on the sides of the bowl. Another way to secure the bowl for adz work is shown in the drawing at right. This bowl-chopping block from the village of Gallejaur in northern Västerbotten allows you to work on the blank as with a chopping block, but without having to hold it with your hand.

The stroke with the adz is that of a pendulum, with your wrist at the center. The knob of the handle is rounded to fit in the palm of your hand, so there is some rotation of the tool at the beginnning and end of the stroke from this center, too. The opposite hand cannot grip the adz handle above the adz hand, as this would inhibit the arc of the stroke. You can add support by grasping the adz hand itself or the wrist of that hand. As when hewing, there is also a more powerful

A bowl chopping block

A hollowing adz excavates the blank, which is held either at an angle on a chopping block (above, left) or secured between dogs on a workbench. The bowl block shown in the drawing supports the blank for two-handed tool use. The low bench (above and left) allows longer strokes than a cabinetmaker's bench would allow. The adz can be supported by grasping the adze hand itself (left) or the wrist of that hand.

one-handed stroke, beginning high up and entering the wood and following through on an arc. Snapping your wrist releases the chip.

Work alternately from both ends to keep from cutting up-grain. You can hollow entirely with the adz, or you can remove the rough waste in the middle with an ax. First cut in with the adz from either end, then chop out the waste with the ax parallel to the sides of the bowl, working from either side toward the middle. As you deepen the hollow, be sure to slope the end-grain walls inward; if you hollow too steeply these walls will be weak. The adz can now carve down one end and along the bottom to meet the adz strokes from the other end. Before you cut too deeply, check the depth of your bowl with a straightedge and ruler, as shown below. When you get used to working with the hollowing adz, you will discover that it is an effective tool for quickly hollowing a blank.

Check the depth of your bowl periodically, using a straightedge and ruler (right). Controlled power with the gouge comes from finding support for your hands against your body, the blank and the bench (below).

Shaping the inside—The hollowing adz has a deeply curved edge and it always leaves some chop marks, so a gouge is used to smooth the shape it creates. There are two technical difficulties when working with gouges: powering the stroke and stopping it. Of course, a gouge can be tapped with a mallet, but this tends to leave a choppy surface. Powering by hand can yield longer, smoother strokes, as long as you can stop the gouge before it begins to cut up-grain. The bottom of the bowl curves into and then out of the grain. In addition, any wavy grain will change direction in a flat surface. The gouge must always cut down-grain or it will tear, so you must be able to stop the stroke precisely where the grain direction changes.

Controlled power with the gouge comes from locking your arms against your sides and/or against the blank and pushing with your entire body. You can also rest your elbow on your hip and power the stroke from there. Your stance, if you are working at a standard-height bench, should be wide, with your right foot back if you are right-handed. Initiate the stroke from your legs. A low bench permits kneeling or sitting, legs still spread wide, and powering the stroke with the upper body. Your force can be more stable with the work positioned higher on your body.

You should have two hands on the gouge, one pushing forward, the other pressing the bevel down as well as resisting too much travel in the stroke. Notice in the photos below and on the facing page how a hand is positioned on the chest, an arm on the knee, or a forearm or wrist on the blank so that the power is controlled through the stroke. Along the sides of the bowl you can hook your thumb or fingers over the rim for guidance, as shown below. You should be able to take repeated cuts at a controlled depth, and stop at the same place each time.

When you can, wrap a finger or fingers around the edge for support.

Roughing the outside—If you are working with green wood, it is best to rough-hew the outside of the bowl as soon as you have hollowed the inside so that the blank will dry more evenly and be less likely to crack. Even so, if you ever put the blank aside for a while, keep it in a plastic bag with some shavings. Shape the rim along the sides first, working from the middle down toward each end. Hew as close as possible to the layout line. Next, chop the corners off the back of the blank, then angle the ends as shown in the photos below. When you've tapered both ends to an angle that corresponds to the end-grain walls on the inside of the bowl, begin shaping the sides of the bowl to match the long-grain walls. You are trying to duplicate the inside shape of the bowl on the outside, and you must stop periodically to test the thickness with your thumb and fingers.

Smoothing the bowl—To smooth the surfaces roughed out by the ax, you can clamp the bowl upside-down on a bench and work it with a splitting knife, drawknife or spokeshave. Position a block of wood inside to support the bowl. Use long strokes to produce a smooth, continuous surface. You can finalize the shape of the bottom at this time.

With the inside roughed out, begin shaping the outside of the bowl by hewing to the layout line.

Taper the ends of the bowl next, first chopping off the corners of the blank, then whatever wood remains until the outside parallels the shape of the inside.

Smooth the outside shape with a splitting knife, drawknife or spokeshave.

Before smoothing the inside of the bowl, it's a good idea to refine the shape of the rim. You can use a block plane or knife for the perimeter, and, with the bowl clamped right side up on the bench, a block plane or spokeshave to smooth the surface of the rim itself. Now you can adjust the width of the rim, making it symmetrical if that is your design, as you smooth the inside of the bowl. Use a wider, flatter gouge than you used earlier, and the gouge marks you leave can be the final surface of the bowl. Aim for long, smooth strokes that produce a pleasantly sculpted surface. Alternatively, you can sand the bowl, but green wood must first be allowed to dry. (See pp. 124-130 for drying and finishing woodenware.)

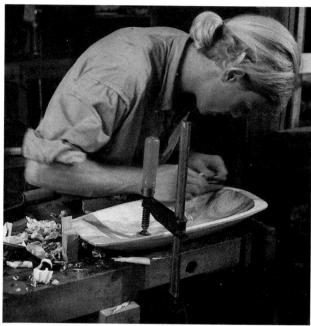

Shape and smooth the rim from the outside in: first the perimeter, then the top. Then fine-tune the width of the rim as you smooth the inside gouge marks with a wider, flatter gouge.

Knife
Grips

A Butter Paddle Making a simple butter paddle is a good way to learn the basic grips and techniques of carving. Utensils should be carved from wood that has substantial tensile strength and is hard, even grained and nontoxic. Birch, juniper, mountain ash, maple and fruitwood like cherry, plum and apple are all fine woods for utensils. Although it's not very hard, birch is a good wood to practice on. Butter paddles made from birch seem to hold up well.

Blanks for butter paddles can be sawn out on the bandsaw or table saw, but a better method is to cut the wood to appropriate lengths and split out the blanks. Splitting them out will make it easy for you to select blanks that are straight grained and easy to carve. All that you need to split out blanks are a knife and a mallet. To avoid damaging the back of your knife, use a rubber mallet, not a hammer.

The function of the butter paddle is most important. You should be able to butter bread with it, it should be able to stand up to substantial use and it should feel good in your hand. The blade of the paddle

Splitting blanks for butter paddles.

should be wide and thin, and the most slender part of the handle should be at least twice as thick as the blade to give it strength. Grain direction and structure ought to figure into your design. Pieces 18cm to 22cm (7 in. to 8⅞ in.) long, 4cm to 5cm (1½ in. to 2 in.) wide and 1cm to 1½cm (⅜ in. to ⅝ in.) thick are appropriate to start with. The approximate shape of the paddle can be drawn on the blank, but let the final shape grow out of the wood during the course of your work. The photo below shows a few different design possibilities.

Principles of carving—Before we go further into carving, it's important for you to understand two fundamental principles: carving down-grain and cutting with edged tools.

You must always carve down-grain and not up into the grain. The drawing at the top of the facing page shows the outline of the paddle divided into sections, and the carving direction is indicated by the arrows. Carving toward point A or E is not difficult, but stopping at point C or G is not so easy. If you do not stop at these points, you will begin carving up-grain and break out wood that was meant to remain a part of the paddle. You must stop where you begin to go up into the grain and cut toward that same point from the opposite direction. Grain direction can also vary on the side and the face of the paddle, especially if there is uneven grain or a small knot present. Sometimes it will be necessary to stop and reverse direction several times as the curve of your paddle crosses the grain direction. Wherever you feel your knife start to dig in, stop and carve toward that point from the opposite direction.

A butter paddle can have various shapes, making it an excellent project on which to practice carving techniques.

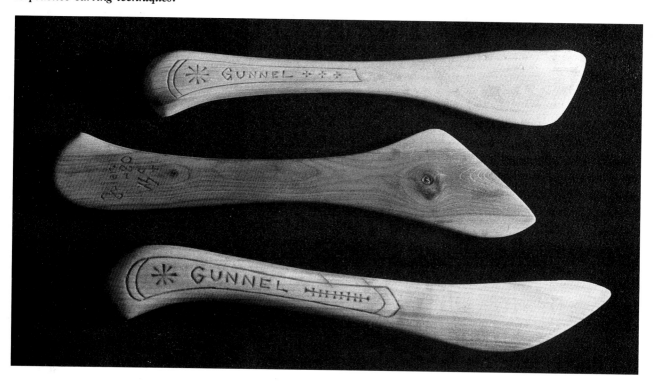

The second principle is that knives and other edge tools cut far better if you slice with them at the same time as you move them forward. If you take a razor-sharp knife, ax or any other edge tool and push the edge straight down on the inside of your fingertip or thumb, you will be able to press quite hard without cutting through the skin. But if, while maintaining that pressure, you make the slightest slicing movement you will surely cut yourself.

Power Strokes
Begin roughing out your butter paddle using power strokes, carving away from yourself. You can use all of your strength with such strokes to waste large quantities of wood. What you cannot do is put on the brakes and stop wherever you want. Thus you can use these strokes only when you are certain that you will be carving down-grain, and there must be plenty of room, with nothing in the path of the knife when it leaves the wood.

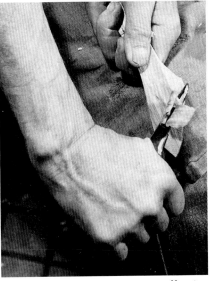

The forehand grip—This is one of the most important and fundamental grips used when carving with a knife. It's easiest to carve when you are sitting, and the hand holding the blank should be supported far forward on your knee, as shown at right. Place the knife on the blank as close to the hilt as possible. Let the knife ride well up in the web of your thumb so that it will angle upward, away from the direction of travel. To get the best shearing effect, let the tip trail so the knife slices from hilt to tip as you push it forward. If you are making heavy wasting strokes, you should have your arm straight so you can push the knife with your shoulder and upper body.

The forehand grip is more effective when the knife is at an angle with the tip trailing.

You can use the forehand grip on the butter paddle when you are carving on the sides, when thinning down the blade and when roughing out between points B and A, H and A, D and E, and F and E.

You can also use the forehand grip and carve against a stop, as shown in the photo at right. The stop could be a clamped piece of wood or a chopping block that will not damage the edge of the blade. When I use this method I am always reminded of something that was quite common during my youth. In logging camps or out in the woods, there was seldom access to dry birch firewood or birch bark. But you could always find a piece of dry pine or a pitchy stump from which

Carving directions on a butter paddle

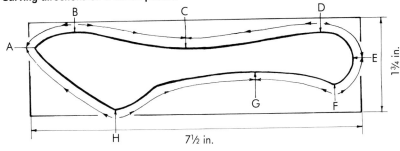

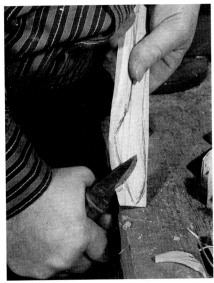

Power can be added to the stroke if you carve against a stop.

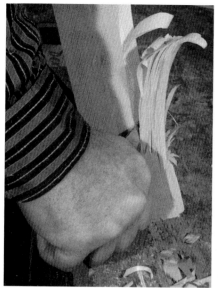

Shaving tinder is an excellent way to practice the forehand grip.

you could shave tinder. As the photo at left illustrates, making tinder was a great way to learn the forehand grip. It was fun and we would compete to see who could make the most shavings without cutting through the butt end of the wood.

The chest-lever grip—The chest-lever grip is another grip with which you cut away from the body. Grasp the knife with the edge turned upward toward the back of your hand. The tip should be tilted slightly downward so that the hilt of the handle is hooked by the joint of the index finger. Grasp the blank in a similar manner with your opposite hand. Now turn the edge of the knife away from you. The blank can remain as is or be twisted slightly into a suitable position for cutting.

Your elbows should be positioned straight out from your sides, as shown below. Place the knife on the blank as close to the hilt as possible, the same as when you began the stroke for the forehand grip. Now pull your hands apart, moving your upper arms and elbows backward at the same time you push your chest forward. Your forearms, hands and wrists act as two levers, and your chest becomes the fulcrum. The cut slides out from the hilt to the tip as the stroke progresses.

Start the chest-lever grip with your elbows almost straight out from the sides, and your hands in contact with your chest. Your forearms, hands and wrists act as levers and your chest as the fulcrum.

This grip and stroke are unusual, but they give you an enormous amount of power when you want to waste wood quickly. Besides the fact that you are using your arms as levers, you gain power from the large muscles of your upper back and shoulders. Obviously, you cannot make long cuts with this grip. This is a safe grip and stroke because the edge and tip of the knife work outward and away from the body, but as in the case of the forehand grip, you must be certain that nothing is in the path of the knife after it leaves the wood.

On the butter paddle, you can use the chest-lever grip in the same places as you do the forehand grip. You should experiment to find what suits you best.

Position of the handle for the chest-lever grip.

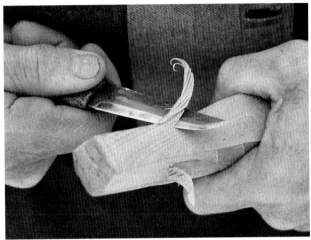
As you use your chest to lever your hands apart, the cut moves toward the tip of the knife.

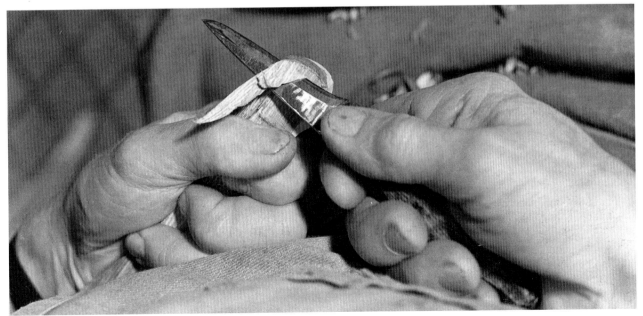
The chest-lever grip as seen from the carver's eyes.

Carving Toward Yourself

When carving and holding the blank with only the help of your hands, you will soon realize that results will be hard to achieve if you carve only away from yourself. On your butter paddle, the areas between points B and D and H and F in the drawing on p. 67 are cases in point. If you are carving away from yourself, you will find it difficult to stop at C or G, or for that matter anywhere else between B and D or H and F. The important contour lines of the object you are carving will also be hard to establish and maintain if you carve only away from yourself. These are cases where you must carve toward the body. This may sound dangerous, but it isn't, provided that you learn how to use your arms, hands, muscles and the blank you are working on to stop the travel of the blade. In most cases the blade will be stopped because part of the knife hand will be resting, or come to rest, against the blank before the blade can leave the wood. In a few cases, the blade will not be permitted to reach the body because of the cocked position of the hands and the locked position of your elbows and forearms against your sides. Therefore, it is necessary to learn the correct grips, strokes and body positions, as well as to be keenly aware of where the knife will leave the wood. When you have mastered the methods, you will be just as safe carving toward yourself as away from yourself. Carving toward yourself also makes it easy to keep your shavings confined to one place.

I'm going to show you six different grips that go beyond the roughing stage of the work, all directed inward or toward the body. I will start with the easier grips and go on to progressively more difficult ones. It's not necessary to know or master all of these grips to finish your butter paddle. All of the grips can be varied and combined to adjust to the object you are carving. You should choose grips and methods that feel good and that seem to fit you best.

The simple pull stroke—Continue with your butter paddle, shaping the line DC. Hold one end of the blank between your thumb and index finger and place the other end firmly against your ribs. The fingers holding the blank should be kept low and out of the path of the knife. With the edge toward you, grasp the knife in your hand with the thumb on the side of the blade, close to the hilt. The thumb will give you the control necessary to adjust the angle of the knife's bevel on the surface of the blank. This is similar to the grip used for honing the right bevel of the knife.

Start the stroke close to the knife handle and slide toward the tip as you pull the knife toward you. This slicing action makes for an efficient cut. As you pull the knife toward you, press your forearms against your sides. Keep your wrists cocked and your elbows locked, and you will be able to control the stroke and stop it anywhere. The support you gain from your body at your waist or lower part of your chest will enable you to carve powerfully or remove fine shavings without losing control of the knife.

Turn the book upside down and look at the photos below to see the hands much as you will see your own hands when carving. You must feel that you have the correct grip and that you always have complete control over the knife and know where the blade will stop. The grip is suitable for making long, controlled strokes that can be started far out on the blank. It does not, however, permit working the butt end that is toward you, because the knife is ultimately halted short of the end by your elbow, forearm and wrist.

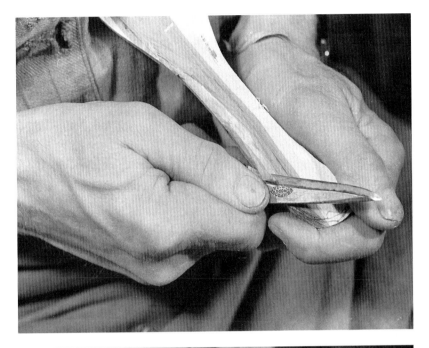

The simple pull stroke is easy to control because the arms are supported against the body. The stroke begins near the knife's handle and stops toward the tip when the wrist meets the body.

The reinforced pull grip—This grip is similar to the simple pull stroke, except that the blank is held by your thumb and index finger, leaving three fingers free to push on the hand holding the knife. This increases the force on the knife and adds control of speed and direction. Because the hand holding the blank is locked in position, long strokes are not possible. Remember to keep your arms pressed tightly to your body and be certain that your thumb and index finger are clear of the cutting edge.

The draw grip—Carving toward the thumb has long been a good method for doing intricate work. The back of the knife is cradled in the four fingers of your hand, while your thumb becomes the steady rest for the blank. The opposite hand clasps the blank between the thumb and index finger. First practice the stroke with your thumb beside the path of the knife, as shown in the photos on the facing page. Squeeze the knife toward the thumb, stopping when the hand is fully closed. It's common to see this stroke with the thumb directly at the bottom of the blank, because with practice you can end the stroke right there.

Keeping your thumb outside the path of the knife will permit slicing strokes. One such stroke can be started close to the hilt, sliding the blade toward the tip as you squeeze the knife toward you and push the blank away. This stroke renders fine results, and mastering it will give you a great deal of satisfaction.

Another way to make a slicing cut with this grip is to start the stroke near the tip of the knife and slide the blade toward the hilt as the knife is squeezed toward you. This method is somewhat easier. Note in the photos on the facing page that the same grip is used for both the knife hand and the hand holding the blank. This time, however, the thumb pushes the blank toward the hilt, instead of away. The movement of the stroke is approximately that of clenching your fist. Make sure that your thumb is well outside the path of the knife.

Reinforcing the pull grip with the fingers of the opposite hand lends power and control to the stroke.

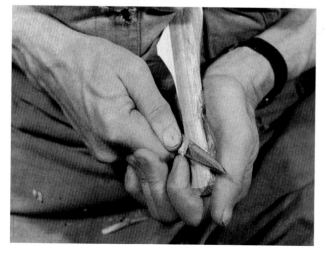
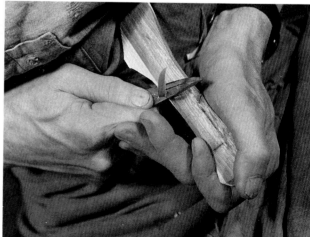

Carving toward the tip of the thumb doesn't give you an enormous amount of power, but it does give you good control of speed and direction. It also permits you to stop where you want to. It's not a dangerous grip, and it's excellent for making fine adjustments and finishing the ends of a blank.

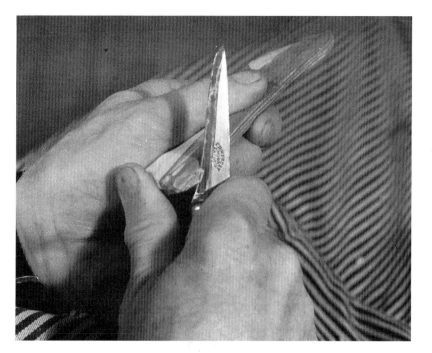

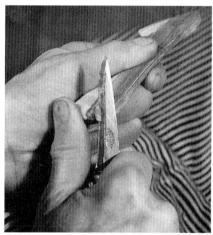

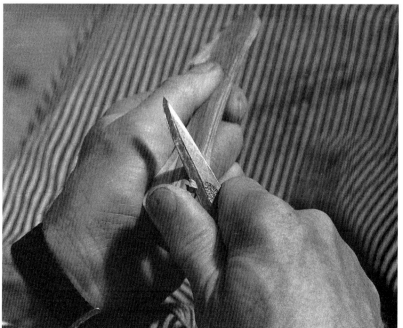

Keeping the thumb outside the path of the blade is a good way to practice the draw grip (top). With care and practice, the blade can be made to stop at the thumb (bottom).

The draw grip cuts smoothest when it's used to shear from the tip of the blade to the hilt (top), or from the hilt to the tip (bottom).

The thumb-joint grip—The draw grips are limited because on long strokes they do not transfer much force to the knife. Much of your strength is used pushing your thumb against the end of the blank. The thumb can be compared to a lever. Power is transferred from the fulcrum all the way out to the tip of the thumb by various muscles. The closer you position a blank toward the fulcrum, the more power you gain. Moving the blank from the tip of the thumb to a spot just below the first joint will increase your power immensely.

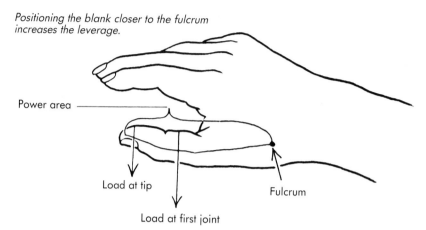

Positioning the blank closer to the fulcrum increases the leverage.

In the thumb-joint grip, the blank is positioned lower down on the thumb. The stroke arcs from knife tip to hilt.

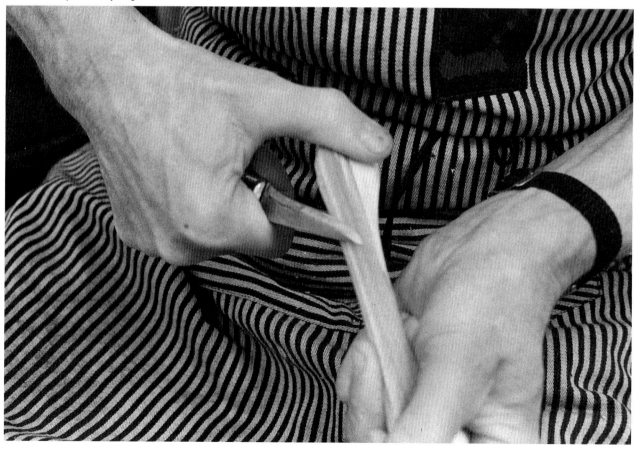

I have seldom seen anyone else using the thumb-joint grip, and I haven't always succeeded in teaching it to others. I'm uncertain as to why this grip is difficult, but it could be due to differences in dexterity, physical makeup or strength.

This grip is similar to the draw grip, except that the blank is positioned slightly below the joint of the thumb, instead of at the thumb's tip. Moreover, the knife is angled toward the blank, and the handle is held across the finger joints, not in the palm of the hand. In this position, a slicing stroke can be made only in one direction from the tip of the blade toward the hilt.

Moving the point of support closer to the hand would seem to shorten the stroke. This is not the case, however, because the fingers can still move sideways, and the other hand can turn the blank into the stroke to lengthen it. Keep in mind that the tip of the knife moves in an arc as you draw your fist tighter. Also, as your fingers tighten, they roll the knife so that it comes to cut along the side of the thumb.

The thumb-joint grip is particularly effective when making smoothing cuts on end grain or carving across the grain. In fact, I know of no other method that combines the power and cutting ability of this grip with complete control of the knife. When carving end grain, it is essential to use a shearing cut to sever the fibers cleanly and leave a shiny surface.

In cases where you need to power a stroke even more, you can move the end of the blank all the way under the second joint of the thumb. This will make you suprisingly strong at the expense of shortening the possible length of the stroke. In the photos below, you can see that the corner of the blank is almost under the knuckle joint and that the edge of the knife is still some distance from the thumb.

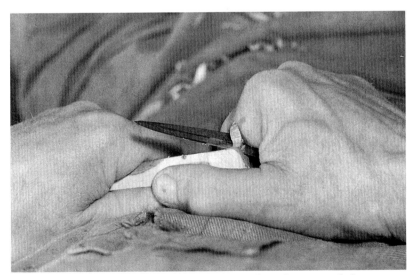

For increased power (in exchange for a somewhat shorter stroke), you can position the blank all the way under the second thumb joint.

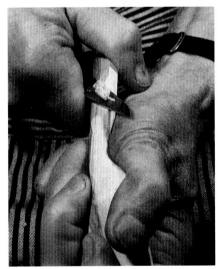

The stop for the thumb-joint grip is your index finger contacting the blank.

The modified thumb-joint grip—Let us look at a variation of the thumb-joint grip. I use this grip along the sides and edges of the blank. Although more difficult than the basic thumb-joint grip, it's very useful. It is especially good when you want to smooth limited areas on an object or gain full control of the knife in difficult grain. It will allow you to carve powerfully, let you stop strokes precisely and give you the finesse you need in finish carving.

The modified thumb-joint grip requires the knife handle to be grasped across your fingers, not in the palm of your hand. When you curl your fingers, the edge should face your thumb.

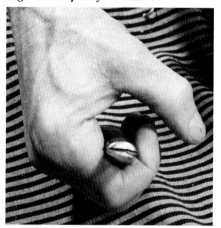

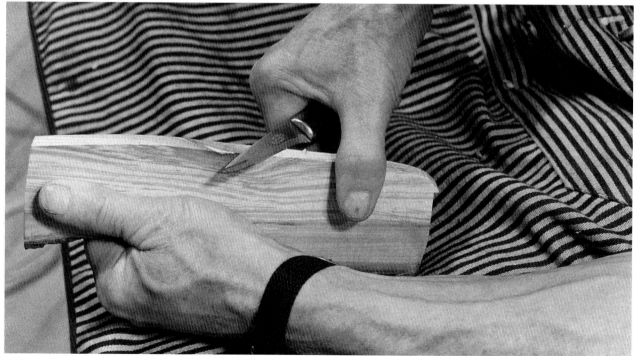

Your thumb must be kept perpendicular to the blank to keep it clear of the blade.

To execute the modified thumb-joint grip, place the knife across your hand and along your finger joints, as shown in the top right photo on the previous page. When you curl your fingers around the handle, the knife blade should be approximately 90° to the back of your hand. Resist the temptation to let the handle slide into your palm.

Hold the blank with your other hand along one edge, and hook the thumb of your knife hand over the other edge of the blank. The angle of your hand in relationship to the blank should be 70° to 80°. It is important that this angle not become more acute because that would force your thumb to rest on its side against the blank. A more acute angle would also change the position of the thumb, putting it in danger of being cut. If the knife is positioned correctly, the bevel should be resting flat on the blank. The stroke is started near the tip of the blade. Sometimes it will be necessary to turn the edge of the blank upward into the underside of your thumb to keep the thumb solidly hooked in position.

During the course of the stroke, the blank is slightly rotated toward the knife hand as the knife hand moves toward the blank. The knife itself moves in an arc from tip to hilt. These movements will make the knife

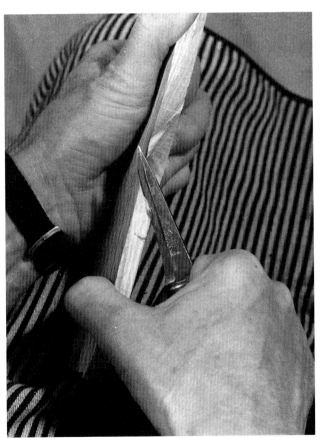 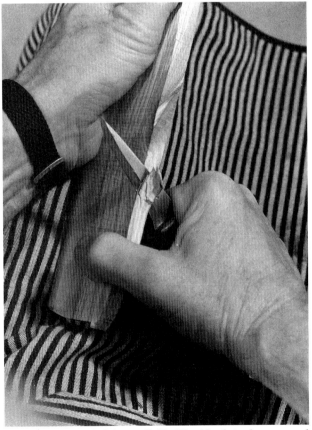

The blank is turned slightly away from the knife to start the stroke near the blade's tip (left). The blank is then rotated into the knife (right), and the stroke is completed when the knife handle and index finger contact the blank.

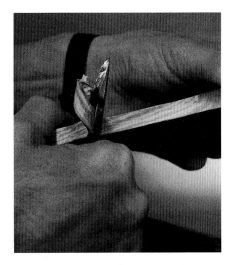

Three more views of the modified thumb-joint grip.

more vertical, which will help you maintain the support of your elbows locked against your sides. A completed stroke should be stopped by the handle of the knife or the index finger meeting the blank before the edge of the knife reaches your thumb.

Even if the knife slips from the wood when you are powering it through a stroke, it should be stopped in the same way. This will be the case only if you are using the correct grip and the correct angles for the stroke. You can also control the movement and stop the stroke at any point along its path. To do this, you should press your elbow and forearm against your rib cage and tense the muscles of your forearm and hand. This will require practice; control is gained through muscular coordination.

The reinforced thumb-joint grip—As with the reinforced pull grip (see p. 72), you can use your opposite hand to add power and control to all the thumb grips, including the draw and modified thumb grips. Begin with the draw grip as described on p. 72, with your thumb supporting one end of the blank. Hold the blank with the other hand between the thumb and upper part of the index finger. You can then use the three fingers you have left to push either on the back of the blade or on the knife hand. This grip allows you to power and steer the stroke with both hands. It will make you twice as strong and increase your control of direction and speed.

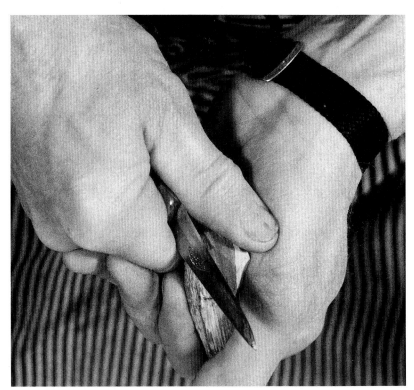

Two hands are better than one. Reinforcing the draw grip with the opposite hand adds control and power.

You can use this grip when you are carving toward the tip of your thumb or toward the thumb joint. The grips and strokes can be varied to suit the blank you are working on. You will learn this through your hands, and by watching and thinking about it. The more muscles that are working together, the more solidly you can hold the blank. This will help you to carve with more precision and safety.

It is usually not necessary to use much muscle when smoothing the wood and making final adjustments to your design. But it is necessary to have solid control of the cutting direction. Use reinforcement from

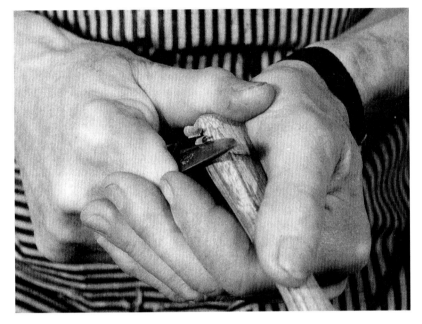

Reinforcing the stroke toward the joint of the thumb.

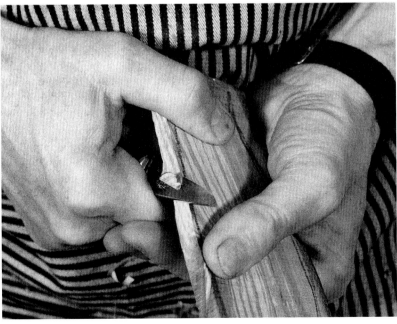

Reinforcing the modified thumb-joint grip with the opposite hand.

the opposite hand to press the bevel of the knife solidly against the blank. If you use a controlled shearing stroke you will be able to create long, smooth surfaces.

A variation of this grip would be to use three fingers of the hand holding the blank to push on the blade, while the little finger presses on the back side of the knife hand, as shown in the photo at bottom left. You can also help the knife hand by giving its thumb a little support with the thumb and index finger of the opposite hand (see the photo at bottom right).

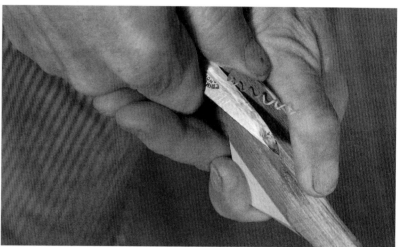

Finish carving requires control that comes from pressing the bevel flat on the work.

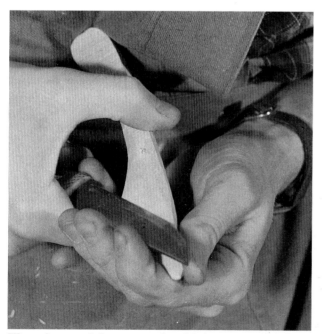

Three fingers of the opposite hand help power the back of the blade. The little finger presses on the knife hand.

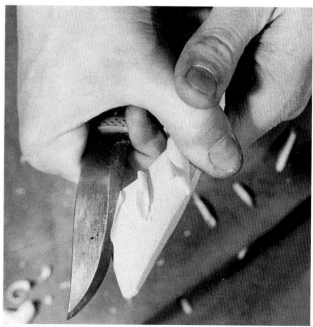

A reinforced thumb grip where both thumbs help to support the knife hand.

Smoothing Strokes

Here are three more grips and several variations on them, from very simple and common to advanced. These tend to be used more at the final stages of a project, when you are smoothing the surfaces. However, they are versatile and frequently handy throughout a project.

The thumb-push stroke — This is an easy stroke, very safe, and useful in smoothing, detail carving and making final adjustments. It is also a good stroke with which to gain dexterity.

The knife should be held somewhat as you held it when grinding. The blank is grasped far forward in the hand. Place your thumb against the back of the knife and begin the stroke close to the tip, and let the knife slice by sliding toward the hilt as it advances. The thumb of the knife hand should support the blade, making it easier to follow through.

This stroke is limited to fine work and does not permit long or roughing cuts. It is excellent when you are carving where you cannot make a mess and wish to direct the shavings into your apron. If you wish to gain more power using this stroke, you can support the front of the blank against a clamped board or chopping block. This will permit you to exert more pressure with the knife hand.

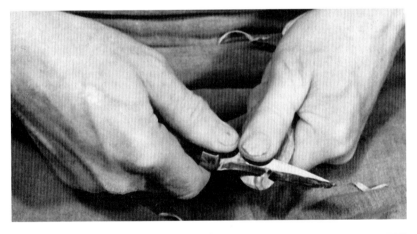

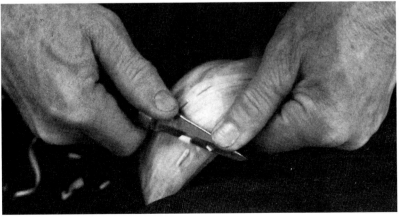

The thumb-push stroke gives good control for finish carving. It also makes it easy to direct shavings into your apron.

When carving a spoon, the transition from the bowl to the stem is difficult, and you must avoid making nicks and deep cuts. The transition should be smooth, as shown in the drawing at left. The photo below left, shows cuts made from the edge of the bowl to the stem that are stopped exactly where they start to go up into the grain. There you must carve from the opposite direction and meet the first cuts exactly. Here the thumb-push stroke will give you the precision to execute these cuts. If you succeed, the transition should look like one clear cut. This stroke is also perfect for crisp detail work, such as ornamentation on a spoon stem.

The wrist grip toward the body—The wrist grip, a more exotic grip, directs the knife and the tip of the blade, though not the edge, toward the body. This may look dangerous, but if the knife is held correctly and the right technique is exercised, it is not. In this case, the wrist is an effective stop when it meets the blank.

This grip has advantages in tight, awkward spots. Because your hand is directly in back of the blade, it is possible to power strokes more than you can with other grips, yet it gives you an enormous amount of control. Here are a few things to think about: The blank you use should be rather long to keep the knife a good distance away from your body. It is an advantage to have strong, flexible wrists. You must always maintain solid support of your lower arms against the front of your body. Take the time to understand and get the feeling of the correct grip and stroke. Concentrate on what is happening and what could happen, that is, where the knife will leave the wood, and where the knife would end up if it slipped.

Carefully observe the position of the hands and the arms in the photo at left on the facing page. Turn the book upside down and look at the picture to get a better idea of how to position your own hands. The

Aim for smooth lines where the grain changes directions, as between the spoon bowl and stem.

Where grain direction changes, smooth the surface with thumb-push strokes, alternating directions.

The thumb-push stroke shapes a hook on the back of a ladle's handle.

blank is held approximately the same as in the simple pull stroke. Angle the hand holding the blank upward to gain the support of the wrist. The tip of the knife is pointed toward the body, while the edge of the knife is away from the body. The palm of the knife hand is turned upward. The knife is clasped with the index finger high up on the handle and the knife angled so that the back of the blade comes closer to the wrist. Unless the handle is too long, try to hook the joint of the thumb over the butt of the handle. The knife hand is also angled to form a less acute angle between the blade and the blank.

Don't forget to press your forearms tightly against your waist and rib cage. Remember, your wrists should be close to each other.

Start the stroke near the tip of the blade, and slice with the tip moving toward your body at the same time the blade is advanced a half inch or so along the blank. The force exerted on the knife is mainly toward your body where the tip is pointing, but when your wrist meets the blank the blade will come to a complete stop. If this stroke is executed correctly, the blade should stop well clear of your body.

The length of the strokes can be as little as ¼ in. to ¾ in., which will necessitate a number of strokes to get you where you are going. Very fine cuts can be longer.

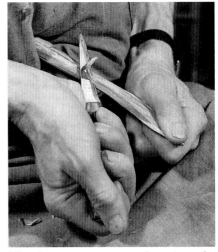

The forearms are pressed against the body and the hands are locked in a cocked position.

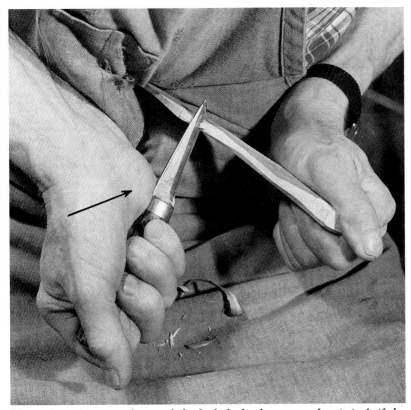

The wrist grip powered toward the body looks dangerous, but it isn't if the correct technique is used.

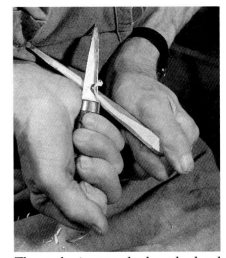

The stroke is stopped when the hand meets the blank.

The wrist grip toward the opposite hand—With this wrist grip, you will be carving away from the body. Grasp the blank between the thumb and index finger, and butt the other end against your stomach, as in the photos below. The blank is supported here to get your hands as close to your knees as possible for safety reasons. The hand holding the blank should be a good distance in front of the knife and as low as possible to stay out of the path of the knife. The knife is held about the same as it was earlier, except that the angle between the blank and the blade is slightly more acute.

The stroke is started by pressing your upper arm against your chest, at the same time as you push your forearm toward your abdomen, hip or thigh. As before, start the stroke near the tip of the blade, sliding it sideways as you push it forward. Retaining pressure on the forearm, let the blade slide forward the length of the stroke.

The brakes and safety in this grip are found in the locking of the muscles in your upper arm and shoulder and in the friction between the arm and body. It is critical that you maintain the pressure of your arm against your body. This will give you the control you need to stop the blade when it leaves the wood, whether by will or by accident.

Remember to keep the bevel of the knife pressed against the surface of the blank to steady the hand and lend precision to this stroke. This grip is unsurpassed when you want to follow the shape of an object in one stroke.

A variation of this technique starts the stroke close to the hilt and lets the blade slide toward the tip. Both wrist grips can be done with the knife edge turned inward toward yourself. You will have experiment to find a suitable cutting angle for the blade.

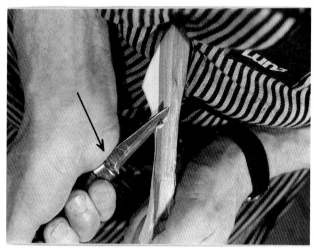

To make this wrist grip safe, it is essential that your hand be cocked and your forearm locked to the side of your body. The hand holding the blank is positioned well in front of the knife hand.

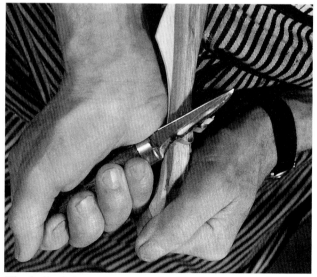

The ball of the wrist meets the blank, stopping the blade short of the opposite wrist.

Finishing the Butter Paddle

To finish the butter paddle, it is not necessary to master all of the grips and strokes that have been discussed in this section. The forehand grip, the simple pull stroke and the thumb-push stroke are all you need to complete your paddle. The forehand grip is fine for roughing out the blank. Both the simple pull stroke and the thumb-push stroke work well for carving down to the final shape and also for doing the finish carving. After you learn these techniques, you may want to practice the reinforced pull grip, the draw grip and the reinforced thumb-grip strokes on your paddle. These three grips are easy to learn after you have mastered the fundamental grips and strokes.

I would suggest that you review the beginning of this section, especially the part on function and proportions of the paddle. Even if a butter paddle is rather flat, try to think of it as the three-dimensional object it really is. It should look proportional from whatever angle you view it. Remove all unnecessary wood, without sacrificing the tensile strength of the paddle.

When doing the finish carving on the paddle, try to get the surface as smooth as possible. If you get it smooth enough with the knife, you may not even want to sand it. If you do choose to sand your paddle, read the section on sanding before you start (p. 124). Finally, you may want to give your paddle some decoration or finishing touches, as described on p. 126. Even if you prefer not to engrave any ornamentation on your butter paddle, I suggest that you sign it by cutting in your initials. Personalizing it in this way is a reward for doing a good job, and it somehow makes your efforts final.

Small Projects

Sharpening a Pencil

It disturbs me that so few people today can do a neat job of sharpening a pencil. It's such a simple task, as simple as opening and closing your hand. One method is to use the draw grip.

Hold the pencil between your thumb and index finger, letting it rest on the side of the first joint of the middle finger. The point should be toward you. The tip of the thumb on your knife hand should be against the middle finger of the opposite hand for support, as shown in the photos below. Let the point of the pencil rest against the side of the thumb. The handle of the knife should lie along the finger joints. Open your hand and the pencil will be positioned close to the blade tip. Close your hand and the blade will slide toward your opposite hand at the same time it slices toward the pencil point. The thumb of the knife hand solidly counters the force of the blade. When you complete the stroke, just open your hand again and you're ready to start a new stroke. The side of your thumb supports the lead so it won't break, allowing you to make long even strokes.

Sharpening a pencil using the draw grip: With the pencil's tip against your thumb, open your hand to start the stroke (left). Clench your fist (right) to complete the stroke.

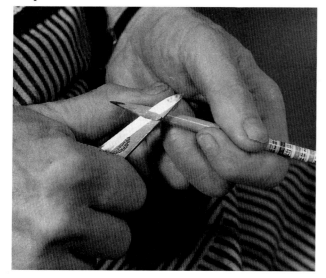 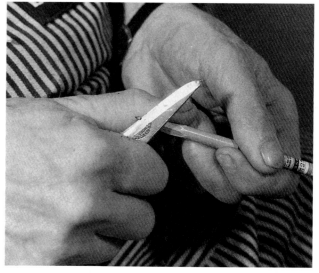

Another way you can sharpen a pencil is to use the thumb-push stroke. The hand holding the pencil supports the point on the index finger and the thumb pushes on the blade, as shown in the photos below. In this case it is the hand holding the pencil that does the work, while the knife hand merely steers the stroke. Notice that the the thumb is positioned near the handle and that the stroke begins close to the tip of the blade.

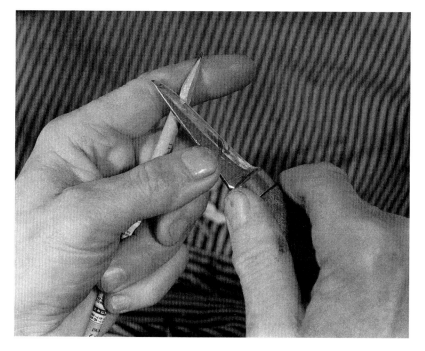

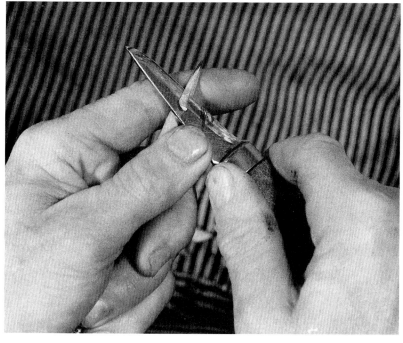

Effective knife strokes incorporate a slicing action. The thumb-push stroke slides the knife from tip to hilt as it moves forward.

Buttons

Wooden buttons make a soft and beautiful finishing touch to clothes that do not have to be washed often. It's fun to choose the wood and fashion the buttons to your own taste. They can be made even more personal by adding your own ornamentation to them.

The procedure is to carve the button on the end of a branch or stick, saw it off and then repeat the process for the next button. This method gives you something to get a good hold of while you're carving. You can use green wood, which is very easy to carve.

Using the powerful forehand grip, the blank is stripped of its bark and carved into round.

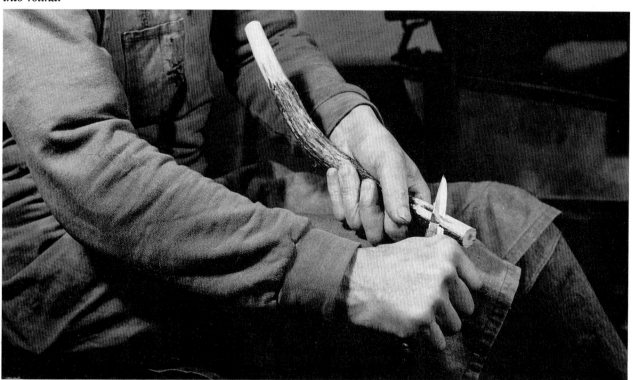

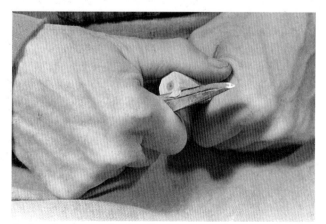

A thumb grip works fine for carving endgrain, which is the show side of the button.

This stroke, which cleans the back of the button, can be made more effective by turning the blank into the knife.

Saplings or branches from dense, tough woods will do fine. Woods with a tendency toward radial cracking or with large piths should be avoided. Lilac has both of these disadvantages, in spite of the fact that it is both beautiful and hard. Birch, juniper, buckthorn, apple, plum, pear and almost any other fruitwood are all fine. You can also try berry bushes and decorative shrubs. If you have larger pieces of wood, you may be able to split them and solve the problem of radial cracking and excessive pith. The splits will have to be roughed down to suitable diameters for making buttons. The blank in the photo on the facing page is from a decorative shrub whose wood is similar to that of the spindle tree (*Euonymus* spp.), a tree or shrub with dense, hard wood sometimes used for making spindles. In Swedish it's called *benved* (bone wood). This piece had been outside for several years with the bark on and had not cracked or become rotten.

Prepare your blank by cutting off a piece to get away from possible end cracks and checks. Using the forehand grip, round the blank evenly. Make the button holes by drilling into the end grain with a 2mm or 2½mm (approximately ⅟₁₆ in. to ³⁄₃₂ in.) twist drill. Try to keep the holes parallel and straight in line with the blank.

Now you can carve the show side of the first button. The best method is to carve toward the joint of the thumb. Start by rounding the surface of the outside edge and working toward the middle. Turning the blank into the edge with the opposite hand will give you a shearing cut that will leave a clean and shiny surface. Other grips, such as the thumb-push grip, will also work, or you can support the end of the blank on a board or chopping block and use the forehand grip.

A good way to practice fine finish carving is to try to get the surface of the button as even and as smooth as possible so you don't have to use abrasives. A carved surface has more life than a sanded surface. But there's nothing wrong with a well-sanded surface, if you prefer.

When you have finished the show side of the button, use a fine-toothed saw to cut it off at whatever thickness you want. The back side can be carved clean or sanded. A knife with a short blade works well. To relieve the edge on the backside, use the draw grip. Last, use a countersink bit spun between your fingers to bevel the holes slightly on both sides. This lessens the wear on the thread.

When your buttons are finished, let them soak in boiled linseed oil for a day or two. Linseed oil without added turpentine will give them a finer lustre. Wipe off the oil on the surface (see the caution on p. 130) and let the buttons dry for approximately 14 days. They then will be ready to sew on your jacket or sweater. The more they wear, the more beautiful they will get.

If you want buttons with a specific color for a special garment, you can add some powdered or oil pigment to the linseed oil. Experiment to get the color you want.

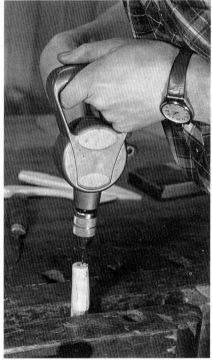

A hand drill can be used to drill the button holes.

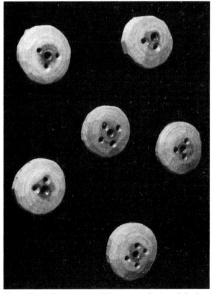

Finished buttons. The number of holes can vary.

A Clothes Hook

At one time or another you will find the need for a strong clothes hook, so why not use the natural hooks in trees to make one? A well-chosen limb, shaped and smoothed by hand, will help make a fitting transition from outdoors to indoors. Blanks can be found wherever trees are felled. Select them before the tree is limbed.

Material for a clothes hook.

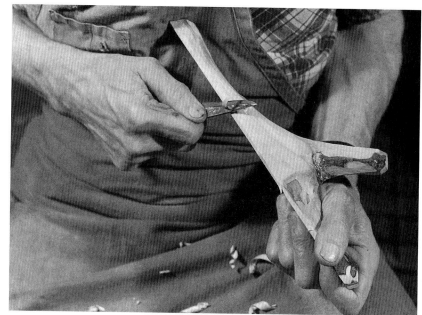

Long pull strokes are used to shape the front of the clothes hook after the back has been planed.

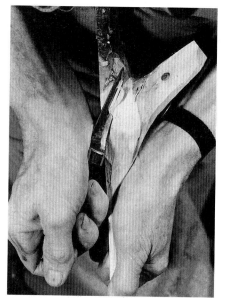

This wrist grip uses the ball of the wrist as a fulcrum, levering the knife through its stroke.

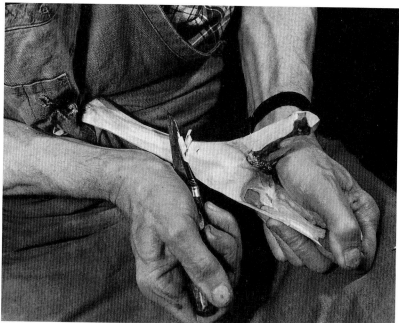

A wrist grip is used to give the blank its final shape.

Split the blank down the pith to get a flat surface on the back side that will be toward the wall. The shape of the hook is up to you. Keep in mind, however, that you should take off enough wood so the hook won't look clumsy, but leave enough on in the right places so it won't lack strength.

The blank shown in the photos on the facing page is birch. Before carving, slightly more than half the diameter was removed on the back side, and then that surface was planed. You should decide the approximate shape of the hook before you begin to work. You can do this by making sketches on paper or by carving models out of small branches. Rough out the shape with a large knife or ax. If you're working green wood, let it dry after you have roughed it out. It's a good idea to rub it with a boiled potato and not expose it to excessive heat. This will help to keep it from cracking and checking.

When you are carving down to the final shape you will have a chance to practice many different grips. The wrist grip used in the bottom right photo on the facing page is described on p. 82. The bottom left photo shows a wrist grip that we did not talk about earlier. Here the knife is not advanced; instead it uses the wrist as a fulcrum against the back of the blank. The strokes are made by levering the knife forward and upward, using the wrist for support.

Starting with your original idea in mind, work toward the final shape of the clothes hook, but don't adhere too stringently to your pattern. You can let the shape of the hook grow out of the blank. You may have to change the shape because of an unexpected defect in the wood or a slip of your knife. Try to get flowing and defined lines, and try to make the sides symmetrical. Symmetry gives you a feeling of peacefulness. If you do prefer to make your hook asymmetrical, be sure to divert from the symmetry enough so the finished object clearly shows your intention. Always work toward a balance between the natural shape and the one created by your hands, and keep in mind the function of the object. Some shapes require you to hold the knife in unusual ways. The more grips and strokes you can practice and master, the greater access you will have to new shapes. Can the figure of the wood lend something to the design? Would it be a good idea to add some kind of ornamentation? Use your imagination and work with your material to express yourself.

The clothes hook shown at right is quite simple with clean lines. Notice how the ends are finished. Although each one is a little different, they both have room for the screws in the final shape. Rounding or beveling the back edge of the clothes hook slightly will accent it when it's mounted on the wall. You can finish up the clothes hook by sanding the surface, or you can take the challenge of finish carving with the knife, as was done on the hook in the photo. Be sure to use a slightly greased, razor-sharp knife with an absolutely flat bevel for the final cleaning up.

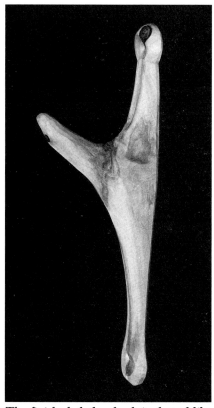

The finished clothes hook is shaped like a large thumb. Screws can be nestled into the holes at either end.

A Peg Board

A peg board doesn't always have to be a machined board with turned pegs. The board can be carved by hand and given a personal touch—a low relief carved into the upper part of it, for example. By carving the pegs, you can give them a shape that takes advantage of the natural strength of your material.

Select a board that is approximately 230mm by 60mm by 11mm (9 in. by 2⅜ in. by ⅜ in.). Plane the board with a finely tuned smooth plane to make sanding unnecessary. Make a pattern on a piece of paper. If you want the board to be symmetrical, fold the paper and draw half the shape up to the fold, cut it out and unfold your pattern.

Drilling the holes is an easy matter. If you use a brace and bit, clamping the board to a stool or chair will give you better control. Keep the bit perpendicular to the board or angled slightly toward the top of it.

The thumb-joint grip, the reinforced pull grip, the wrist grip and the reinforced draw grip are some of the grips you will have use for when shaping the board. It will sometimes help if you can support the board

Shaping a clothes peg for strength

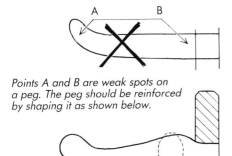

Points A and B are weak spots on a peg. The peg should be reinforced by shaping it as shown below.

The layout for the peg board's shape is made directly on the blank.

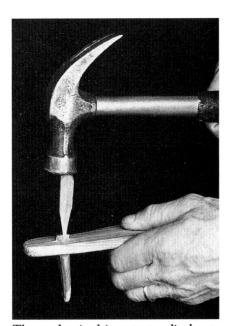

The wedge is driven perpendicular to the board's grain direction.

To shape the edge of the board blank, you can saw relief cuts, then use a modified thumb-joint grip and shear from blade tip to hilt.

against a solid object. The entire edge can be rounded, or, as in the bottom right photo on the facing page, made at a right angle to the board and then relieved or beveled.

The pegs can either be split out of a larger piece of material the same length as the length of the pegs, or rough sawn out of a board of suitable thickness. A coping saw or fine turning bowsaw can be used to saw out the blanks. Use a bench vise if you have access to one, otherwise clamp the board to a sturdy chair.

Small pegs can be hard to work with. You can make a handle by using the same bit you used to drill the tenon holes. Drill a hole in the end of a piece of waste and chuck the peg-blank tenon into it.

Garments should hang far out on the pegs so they get air around them. A little hook or knob will keep clothes from falling off. Shapes facilitating these functions are often found on older carved pegs. When carving the pegs, keep in mind grain direction and tensile strength. Because the strain on the peg is greatest at the surface of the board, it's a good idea to widen the hole slightly from the front surface with your knife or a tapered reamer. Taper the tenons to match.

Practice different grips and strokes when you are carving the pegs. You can start by wasting wood toward the tip of the peg with the forehand grip. The draw grip and carving toward the joint of the thumb are good grips to use for the hook. Don't forget that you can vary and combine grips to suit yourself and the object you are carving.

After applying glue to the tenon and the hole, turn the peg into position. Make certain that the hook of the peg points upward, and check that all the pegs angle out uniformly. Don't try to wipe off the squeeze-out. Let it skin over first, then remove it with a chisel and the tip of a knife, but be careful not to damage the surface of the board.

Wedge the tenons from the backside immediately after glue-up. Start the split for the wedges with a chisel that is the same width as the diameter of the tenon. The wedges should be carefully tapped in at a 90° angle to the grain direction of the board (across the grain). They should be of wood that is about the same hardness as the wood used for the pegs. Make the wedges long enough so they will be easy to work with. After the glue is dry, cut off the tenons and wedges flush with the board using a fine-toothed saw or your knife.

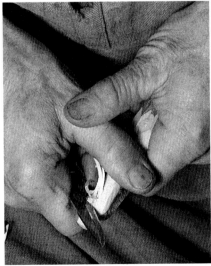

An auxiliary handle (left) helps you get a grip on the peg when shaping it. Carve the contour behind the peg's tip using a thumb-joint grip.

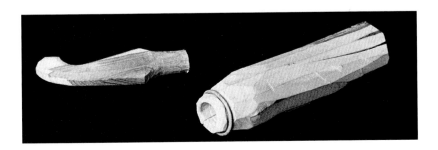

Carving Spoons

Form and Function

In recent years I have come across many badly designed wooden spoons and ladles. I'm sure that these are done in good faith, but the results are wrong. Most of the time the mistakes are due to lack of knowledge, but sometimes they are the result of trying to be arty. Wooden spoons should be made to use, not to hang on the wall. Combining good materials with good functional design will result in beautiful, practical objects.

A fine ladle made of apple wood for small pots.

A wooden spoon should fit the hand and be functional as well as beautiful.

Unfortunately, the use of wooden spoons has all but disappeared. One reason for this is that most people don't know that you can eat with them. Wooden utensils are regarded as things of the past unable to meet today's hygienic standards. Thus, there is no demand for them. Almost no one wants to pay for the training, artistic intuition and craftsmanship it takes to make them.

Wooden spoons and ladles represent a refined attention to the combination of form, function and materials. They should be made of good wood—even grained, odorless and with high tensile strength—and with no extra wood because spoons should be light. They should also be durable, shaped not only to withstand long, regular use, but to invite it; they should be pleasurable to use. You can eat quietly with a wooden spoon without being disturbed by harsh sounds. Kitchen spoons can be shaped for turning, scraping and serving. And of course, wooden spoons can be washed. Preparing, serving and eating food with wooden spoons and ladles is a wholesome experience, especially if you make your own spoon or receive one as a gift. And when a spoon shows the care and skill necessary to carve it, it gives back each day it's used the spirit that went into making it.

Spoons can take on a variety of shapes when function is balanced with the material and personal expression. In the photo at top, the small scoop (about 3 in. long) is from birch burl, the stirring spoon is from crooked bird cherry, and the ladle is from birch; above, a small spoon; and at right, two table spoons made from straight-grained wood.

Spoons — The blank for a really good spoon should be found with the proper bend already in it, selected from wood that grew that way. Sometimes this is not possible and you will have to use straight-grained wood. In that case you will have to make adjustments to the material at hand to compensate for less tensile strength. The drawing at left, below, is somewhat exaggerated, but it illustrates a number of possible mistakes that can be made on a spoon carved from straight-grained wood:

1. The end of the handle is too thin and will break easily.

2. This part of the handle is too thick. Because the grain is straight, there is already sufficient strength here. A thick handle like this is clumsy to hold.

3. This is the part of the spoon that needs the most strength. A stem this thin will not stand up to much use.

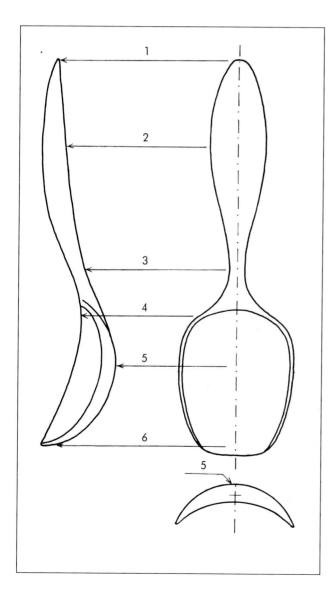

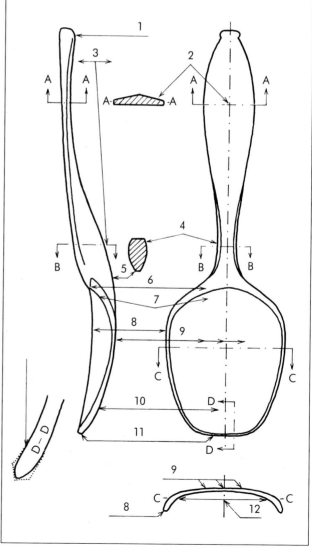

4. These upper edges of the bowl are made too thin. Usually there is weak end grain here, and therefore the bowl should be thicker toward the stem.

5. Where the grain direction is straight, it is not necessary to make the bowl very thick.

6. The lip of the bowl should be thin to make it easy to pick up food or liquid. But in this case the front of the bowl is angled upward too much in relation to the stem. This means that there will be weak end grain here. The error is increased when the lip is carved so thin.

When teaching manual arts, I often make spoons and ladles from straight-grained material. I always choose maple because it is the hardest and most close-grained wood found in Sweden. Even when working with straight-grained wood, it is necessary to take into consideration grain direction as much as possible. The drawing at right on the facing page shows a design that will work well in straight-grained wood. Notice that the angle of the bowl in relation to the stem is not very great.

1. The end of the handle is thick, to add strength in the end grain.

2. The handle can be made wider at this point. This will make it comfortable to hold and strong where it's thin. Rounding or beveling the edge of the handle (cross section AA) will make it look thinner without making it much weaker.

3. This is the part of the spoon that will receive the most stress. To increase the tensile strength here, it's necessary to make the stem thick (cross section BB). Notice that the thickest part is oriented at 90° to the bowl.

4. Slightly rounding or beveling the stem will add to the contrast between thick and thin in the design and will not weaken it much.

5. The bottom of the stem plays an important role in attaching it to the bowl. Notice how it extends underneath the bowl, like a spine or keel, to support and stabilize it.

6. The rear edge of the bowl should be thick to transfer strain between the bowl and stem. Here, the function of the spoon is not hampered by thickness.

7. The rear of the bowl should be steep to give the spoon greater capacity. The upper part of the rear of the bowl will be end grain, and therefore should be relatively thick. The wood can be thinner where the curve of the bottom parallels the grain.

8. The side walls of the bowl can be made quite thin and steep, because they follow the grain (cross section CC). They should, however, have stability, because they are walls.

9. The actual bottom of the bowl follows the grain and is seldom subject to wear. Because of this, the bottom can be made very thin without endangering its strength. How thin will depend on the strength of the wood you are using.

10. The forward wall of the bowl is subject to much wear and strain. In spite of that, it should be thin enough to pick up food easily.

Therefore, you should use a shallow angle here when you are using straight-grained wood. This will leave fairly long fibers and permit you to make the forward wall rather thin.

11. The leading edge is also subject to punishment. This is the part of ladles and spoons that often breaks first. Look at the enlargement of section DD. When you are doing the final carving, make certain you leave enough wood by first creating the shape indicated by the dotted lines. Then softly round the lip.

12. The side walls of the bowl should be angled enough to make generous room for your mouth. If the spoon is too deep, your upper lip will not reach the bottom. Spoons for yogurt can be made shallower than spoons for soup.

This rather complicated description of the engineering of a wooden spoon may seem overly extensive. At first sight, wooden spoons look simple, and as tools for eating, they are. But making them look simple, yet strong and comfortable enough to function well is the result of good design and close attention to detail.

An old traditional spoon was used as a model for this drawing. This spoon has peaceful, beautiful symmetry, but the sketch should not be taken as a universal plan for spoons. Stems can be made longer or shorter, or can vary in both thickness and width. There are an infinite number of ways to vary the end of the handle. The bowl can be larger or smaller, and the proportions between width and length can be altered. The shape of the bowl can be round, more pointed toward the back edge, oval, pear shaped, or open like a shovel. The proportions must, however, be in agreement. The general design has evolved through centuries of human innovation, but the local and individual variations are many.

Once, at a local workshop for craftsmen, an instructor suggested that one of the participants make a design change in his project. Somewhat insulted, the man exclaimed, "Do you mean that we all should do everything exactly alike?" That question could be relevant in many situations. I would answer this way: The point is certainly not that all objects look alike. They must, however, follow the laws that the material and function dictate. The special laws of form and proportion should enhance and strengthen the function of the object. After these criteria are met, there will still be plenty of room left for local and individual variation.

Ladles — What is the difference between a spoon and a ladle? The main difference is their size. If a spoon is too big to eat with because the bowl won't fit your mouth or if the handle is long, you can call it a ladle. Traditional Scandinavian ladles are multipurpose utensils. They are used to stir and serve food and to scrape the bottom of the pot. Some of them may have specific purposes, such as soup ladles, gravy dippers or salad servers. Soup and gravy ladles obviously require deeper bowls set at a sharper angle to the stem.

Two views of a birch ladle with a hook that makes room for your fingers (left), and a pair of salad servers (below).

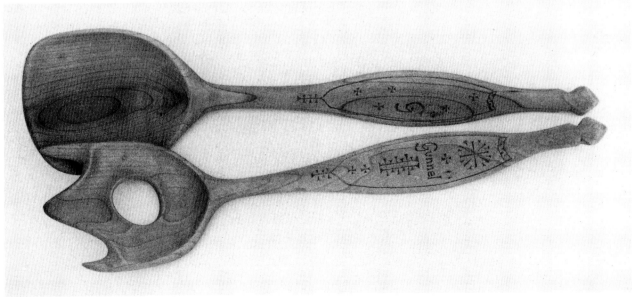

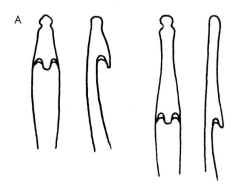

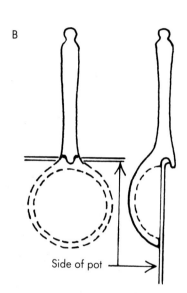

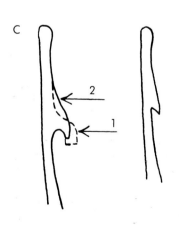

Side of pot

Ladle hooks can have an infinite number of design solutions. However, it is essential to leave more wood where there is end grain. The hooks should look more like the hook at arrow 2 than at arrow 1.

Ladles are often given hooks so they can be hung on the side of the pot or kettle. The hook can be located almost anywhere along the stem or handle, as in drawing A at left. If the hook is located at the end of the handle, make sure that there is enough wood left behind it for strength where there is weak end grain. The hook can be far down on the stem so your hand will fit above it. Located there, the hook will be strong. The hook can be made large enough so you can get your index finger under it, to give you a good grip on the ladle. In southern Sweden, some ladles are made with the hook on the front side, above the bowl, as in drawing B.

If the hook is too long and fits the kettle tightly, it is apt to break. The hook at arrow 1 in drawing C makes the transition from hook to handle too abruptly, leaving little wood to reinforce the weak end grain. The hook does not have to be wide, but it must have a sufficient amount of wood attaching it to the handle, as at arrow 2.

Instead of making rounded hooks, you can make an angled notch on the handle, as in drawing D. This is the way to go if you want to make a number of quick ladles.

Carving Spoons and Ladles   It's simply

impossible to meet all the criteria for a good spoon or ladle if you are working out of straight-grained wood. You will always end up with end or sloped grain somewhere. Only if you find a crook that follows the curve of the handle, stem and bowl will you be able to make a really graceful and strong spoon or ladle.

Finding a spoon in a tree—All crooks are not appropriate for spoons. Many of them are twisted or have too wide a curve, and you may end up with a faulty shape or more end grain than if you had used straight-grained wood. A spoon or ladle made from a crook like the one in the drawing at left on the facing page would not be good. It would roll over in the pot and not fit your hand.

Look for a rather sharp crook in the trunk of a sapling or limb to find an ideal spoon or ladle blank. Locate the back of the bowl immediately before or after the steepest part of its curve, as illustrated in the middle drawing on the facing page. A spoon made from a crook like this will feel good in your hand. Preferably use a blank that is completely free of knots. Sometimes you can find good spoon blanks where the limb is attached to the trunk of the tree, as in the drawing at right on the facing page. In this case, you would use the bottom half of the limb for the handle and stem, and the trunk for the bowl.

Splitting the crook with an ax—When you find a suitable crook, you should split it along its pith, following its curve. Any remaining pith should be removed with an ax or knife, because including the pith makes the blank prone to cracking.

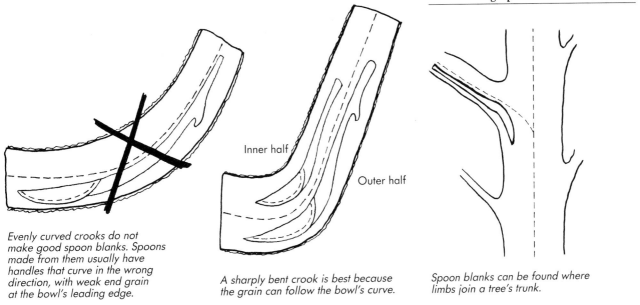

Evenly curved crooks do not make good spoon blanks. Spoons made from them usually have handles that curve in the wrong direction, with weak end grain at the bowl's leading edge.

Inner half

Outer half

A sharply bent crook is best because the grain can follow the bowl's curve.

Spoon blanks can be found where limbs join a tree's trunk.

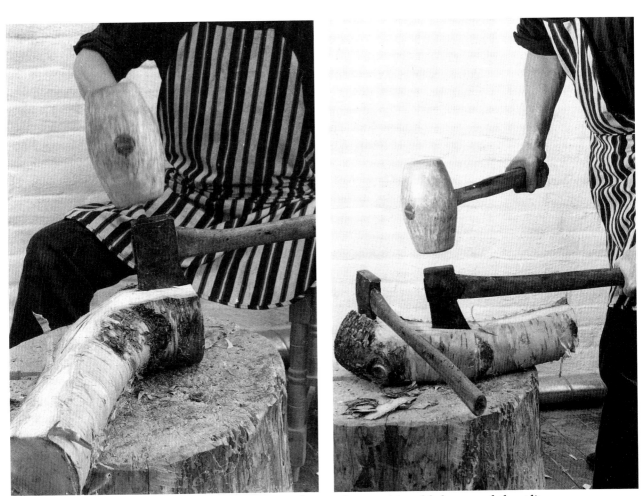

A crook can be split using an ax as a wedge. A second ax at the opposite end helps control the split.

Before you split the crook, remove the bark from its sides. This will make splitting easier and also let you see where the split is going. Use a wooden maul to drive the ax like a wedge. Start the split by driving the ax into the short end of the crook where the bowl part of the blank will be. Try to get the split to go through the pith. If you don't hit the pith on the first try, move the ax over a hair and try again. Difficult crooks can be split with two axes, one from either end. If you run into interlocked or twisted grain, you will have to crosscut the fibers that run out with an ax. Not doing so will result in a twisted blank.

After you split the crook and remove the bark, you will have to decide whether you can use both pieces or not. A suitable blank should be free from pith, and have no knots, checks or cracks. Its curve will dictate the curve of the handle, stem and bowl of the spoon you intend to make. Make sure there is enough wood to give the bowl proper width and depth. The inner half of the crook will necessarily yield a smaller bowl, because it is rounded in the opposite direction as your bowl will be. If you are working with an ax, you will be able to get only one blank from each half of the crook. By using a turning saw or bandsaw, you may be able to get several blanks from each crook half.

Roughing out the blank with a saw—A turning bowsaw with a narrow ripping blade can be used to saw down the pith of a crook, instead of splitting it with an ax. A bench vise is a great help to hold the crook firmly while sawing. If you don't have access to a vise, you can make do by clamping the crook to a chair or bench.

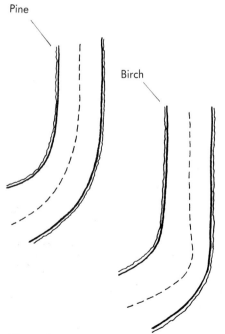

Pine

Birch

The pith usually follows the middle of a pine crook, but in birch it tends toward the outer part of the elbow.

Keep in mind that the pith in birch does not usually follow the curve of the crook. Instead, it takes a sharper turn toward the outside of the elbow, as shown in the drawing and photo on the facing page. Pine's pith runs more consistently through the center of a crook. You will have to guess where the pith runs in your crook and mark out the cutting line on its side. If you end up with the pith on the wrong side of the piece you are going to use, remove it with the saw or ax.

If you don't have a turning bowsaw you can use a rip saw to cut down the straight sections of the crook. Saw to a point slightly short of where the stem of your spoon will be attached to the bowl. Make a similar kerf cut on the bowl end, then use one or more wedges to split the crook.

You now have two spoon blanks, each of which can be secured upright in a vise and the outline of a spoon sawn with a turning bowsaw. A relief cut where the bowl meets the handle will make sawing easier.

Rough out a spoon blank with a turning bowsaw.

Roughing out the blank with a bandsaw—The bandsaw is an especially good alternative if you intend to make a large number of spoons or ladles. It is, however, important to remember that when bandsawing irregular shapes you must have solid support from the table to keep the object from self-feeding and rolling into the blade. Feed slowly and don't force the blade. Make sure your blade is narrow enough to negotiate the curve you want, or make relief cuts. Maintain a wide solid stance. Your hands should be out of the path of the blade, preferably in back of it. Keep your forearms in contact with the table for support, and use the edge as a stop so your hand can't reach the blade. Maintain a solid, but not cramped grip on the blank.

Bandsaws give a false sense of security because of their low rpms. But if they do hook into an object and pull it into the blade, they are unforgiving, and will eat flesh and bone just as soon as they will wood.

Before ripping the crook in half, hew a flat on one side, so the crook will be stable through the cut. With the crook on this flat, begin ripping it down its pith. As soon as enough wood has passed the blade, grasp it first with one hand in back of the blade, later with both hands, and pull the crook through its length. You will now have an inner and outer half of the crook.

The inner half of the crook will be easier to bandsaw than the outer half. This is because you will have a bearing surface along the entire curved, sawn surface of what will become the backside of the spoon. With chalk or a felt marker, draw the rough outline of the spoon's shape on the bark side of the inner crook. Saw the waste from the sides, trying to keep the bearing point of the blank directly under the teeth of the blade.

On the outer half of the crook, the rough outline of the blank is also drawn on the bark side, but this time you will not be able to maintain a bearing surface directly under the teeth of the bandsaw blade. You

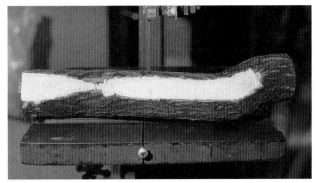

Before bandsawing the blank in half, hew a flat on one side for the blank to rest on through the cut. Then rip the blank down the pith, grasping it securely away from the blade. Note how the forearm rests on the bandsaw table for added stability.

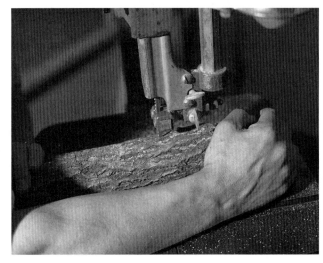

should therefore trim a flat where the leading edge of the bowl will be. This will be your main bearing surface on the table when sawing the outline of the spoon blank. Begin at the bowl end, taking small bites, until you have sawn the rough outline of the bowl. Then you will be able to keep the bearing surface securely on the table as you grasp the bowl in back of the blade, and pull the blank through the cuts on

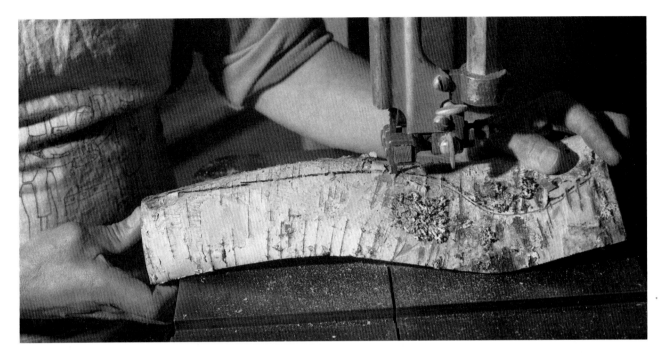

Bandsawing the plan view of the spoon on the inner half of a crook. First one hand, then both are positioned on the far side of the blade to pull the blank through.

either side of the handle. There will be air under the blade along much of the length of these cuts. On large ladles, the bowl end will slide off the edge of the table, but then you will bear on the sawn upper side of the spoon's handle.

With the outline sawn, you saw the contour of the spoon as seen from the side. Draw this contour on one side of the blank. When sawing, you will get support on the table from the sawn side of the bowl and the handle end, but again, you will have air under the teeth of the blade, so keep the blank firmly on the table. Now the blank is ready for knife work.

Roughing out the blank with an ax—Roughing out a spoon blank with an ax requires some practice to do well, but it is not dangerous if you follow proper procedures, and it does give you very direct control of the shaping process. A sense of design that comes from using simple tools cannot be had from machines.

You can use almost any kind of ax or hatchet, so long as it is ground with flat bevels, preferably with the one on the side of your work wider than the other. Because the blank is small, attention to safety is especially important: keep in mind where the ax will end up if it follows through, or strikes a glancing blow. The hand holding the ax should be close to the surface of the block. This will help ensure that the ax will end up in the block and not in your leg if something should go awry. For the same reason, the blank should be supported on the far side of the block.

When the outline is complete, you can saw the contour of the spoon as seen from the side. Again, solid support for hands and stock is essential when bandsawing irregularly shaped stock.

The photos below show the initial work of shaping an inner crook. The side being hewed will become the bottom side of the spoon. At this stage you are mainly cleaning up the split surface, making sure there is no pith.

The next step is to shape the top side of the spoon, in this case, the inner side of the crook. This can be done with an ax, but you may find it easier to control the depth of the cut by first making several relief cuts down to a line before hewing away the waste, as shown in the drawing at right. The photo below, right, shows removing the kerfed waste with a chisel.

Note that when you are using the inner part of the crook, most of the waste is removed from the upper side of the spoon. This means that the bottom and leading edge of the bowl can be made very thin and graceful without sacrificing strength, because the grain follows the shape of the bowl there. The blank will become less crooked as you remove wood. How much less will depend on the depth of the bowl.

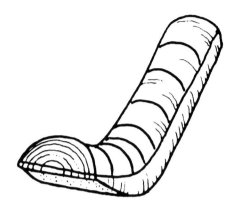

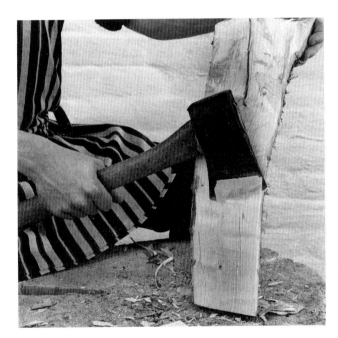

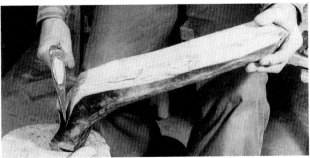

Cleaning up the split on the inner half of a crook. Notice how close the ax hand is to the chopping block.

Relief cuts make it easier to hew to a line without splitting wood that should be saved. The chisel shown here is an alternative to the hewing hatchet.

When the top side has its approximate shape and the blank's thickness is fairly even, you should draw a straight line down the middle. Sight from one end to the other to get the line straight. This line will serve as a reference to work out design and symmetry.

Design and shaping—In determining the shape of your spoon or ladle, consider its specific function and the particular piece of wood you're making it from. You work toward a consciously defined design, but at the same time you exercise flexibility, like an artist making a sculpture. If you work with clay, you can add some more if some is missing. This is not possible with wood. You may at times be able to mend a crack or repair a mistake, but most of the time you must remedy problems by making design changes.

Before you start this next phase of the shaping, examine spoons or ladles that are similar to the one you intend to make. Study the pictures and drawings of spoons and ladles in this book. Then turn to

Once the blank has been brought to rough thickness, sight a reference line down the center to help you in shaping the spoon.

your blank and try to transfer to it what you have learned. Your spoon or ladle will not be exactly the same as its model. Look at your blank from many different directions as you work on it, and the many views you see will help you shape it.

Shaping with the ax—After you have drawn the shape of the spoon or ladle on the blank, you can rough it down further with the ax. You are now beginning to shape the actual plan view of the spoon. To avoid unwanted splitting and make it easier to hew, it's a good idea to make a couple of relief cuts with a saw where the handle will meet the bowl, as shown in the photo below, left. Still, work carefully with the ax. It is very easy as you hew down the side of the handle to go too far and initiate a crack in the bowl.

Hewing the handle in the other direction is easier. Always work below the hand that is holding the blank; don't try to start strokes on the end grain of the handle.

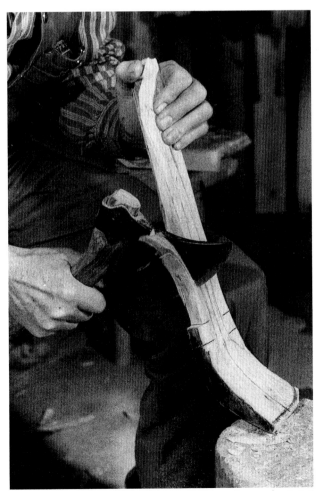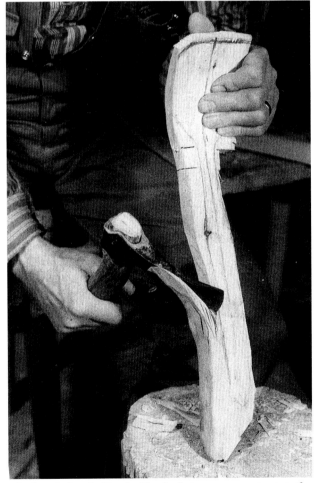

As you shape the plan view of the spoon, always work below the hand that holds the blank. It is necessary to stop the stroke short when working toward the bowl area (left). Even when aided by relief cuts, be cautious. The smallest crack in the bowl can necessitate a major design change.

The back of the bowl can be shaped holding the blank in a couple of different positions. The top photo below shows the bowl being secured on the corner of the chopping block, which offers support behind the short, mincing strokes. To get at the opposite side, turn the blank end for end, grab the handle and position the blank similarly on the corner

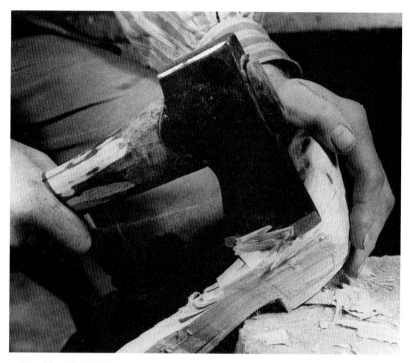

Two grips for rough shaping the backside of the bowl. Notice in both photos how the blank is securely supported on the corner of the chopping block directly below the ax stroke.

of the block. To shape the rest of the bowl back, hold the blank upright, as in the bottom photo on the facing page, and hew toward the leading edge of the bowl. Don't waste away too much wood here. The final shaping of the backside will be done after you have hollowed out the bowl.

Rough shaping with the knife—Whether you've roughed out your spoon blank with an ax or a saw, it's time to switch to your knife to do the final rough shaping. I usually start by roughing down the handle on the back side, which leaves the initial reference line and outline on the upper side of the blank. If you have hewn away part of the outline, redraw it to get the shape back into proportion. Where you are certain you won't carve into the grain, you can use the forehand grip, slicing toward the handle end. The chest lever grip is also fine for this purpose.

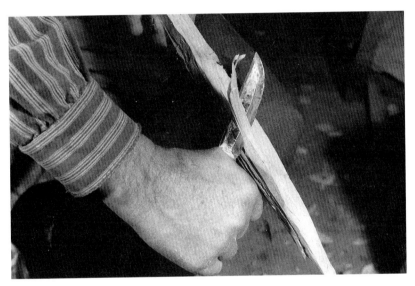

Rough out the spoon handle with the forehand grip (above left) and the chest-lever grip (left).

A modified thumb-joint grip works fine for rough shaping the handle toward the bowl, where strokes without stops will not work. You can further refine this area with the reinforced pull grip or the pull stroke. If you use the pull stroke, maintain good control and be careful not to follow through and cut into the grain on the backside of the bowl. If you are working with green wood, remember to leave plenty of wood on the blank. This is especially important along the stem, so you can make adjustments for warpage or twist after the blank is dry.

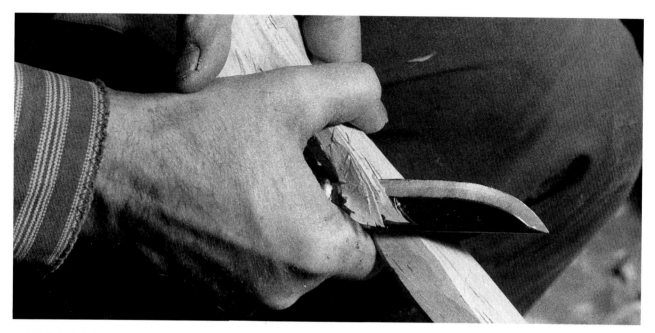

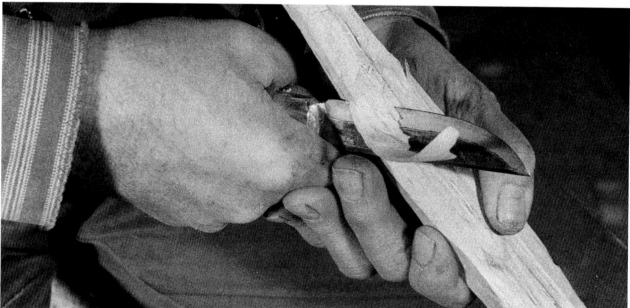

Carve toward the stem with a thumb-joint grip (top). A reinforced pull grip works well to refine the surface along the handle's length (above).

When you are satisfied with the back of the handle, turn the blank over and carve down to the outline of the plan view. The simple pull stroke is excellent for trimming from the middle of the handle to the butt on one side, and from the middle of the handle toward the bowl on the opposite side. You can use this stroke to complete the entire outline if you turn the blank over and carve from the opposite side, but then you will not see the drawn line. You will have to take small cuts and make frequent checks to make sure you stay shy of the line. You may choose to use wrist grips instead, because they will let you carve the entire outline without turning the blank over. If your design is symmetrical, you can develop a knack for carving one side to match the other even when the outline is not visible.

When you are through with the initial shaping of the handle and stem, you can trim the end of the handle by carving toward the joint of the thumb, as seen in the section on buttons (p. 88). You can also do this by using the thumb-push stroke or by supporting the butt against a board or chopping block and using the forehand grip.

If you have a lot of wood left on the leading edge of the bowl, rough it down using the forearm grip or the chest-lever grip. You can also use the thumb-joint grip and the thumb-push stroke. But again, don't remove much wood at the bottom of the bowl until you've hollowed it.

Round the bowl somewhat toward the stem, leaving enough wood where the stem attaches to the bowl for a reinforcing spine that will extend well up onto the bowl bottom. The thumb-push stroke, the simple pull stroke and the reinforced pull grip will all work fine here.

After you have roughed out the backside of the bowl, trim its perimeter down to the outline of the plan view. Here you can switch between using the simple pull stroke, the reinforced pull grip, the thumb-push stroke and the thumb-joint grips. You should carve carefully, being aware that you will have to change carving direction as soon as you start carving up into the grain. Where and how often will depend on your particular blank and the contour of its plan view.

Work now on the relationship between the stem and the bowl: it should be even, though not finished, with no twist in the planes. It can be flattened and straightened out with the forearm grip. On a green-wood blank, you may have to make this correction again if it warps or twists when drying. If the transition from stem to bowl plane is uneven, the thumb-joint grips can be used to work from the stem to the bowl area. You can use the thumb-push stroke all the way to the leading edge of the blank for fine tuning. The simple pull stroke will also work here. The thumb-joint grips can be used, even across the grain, to flatten the bowl close to the leading edge. Be careful when you carve the corners at the leading edge. Here you may start cutting into the grain and split wood that should be part of the rim. This will be especially true if you are working out of straight-grained wood.

Bowl layout—Before you can start hollowing the bowl of your spoon, you need to re-establish some reference lines because you've likely carved them away. With a flexible metal or plastic straightedge or the edge of a heavy piece of paper, find the center of the blank and draw the centerline. Work out the shape of the bowl from this reference line, and draw the shape on your blank. This can be done freehand, with the help of a compass or dividers, or with a pattern made from paper or cardboard.

Hollowing with a carving hook—A double-edged carving hook gives you the advantage of having both a right and left hook in the same tool. I prefer to have two single-edged hooks because it makes it possible to use a greater number of grips. Using the thumb-push stroke (shown below) or using the thumb as a fulcrum for making rounded strokes would not be possible with a double-edged hook.

The hollowing of the bowl is started with a left-edged carving hook, as shown in the photos at left on the facing page. The handle of the hook

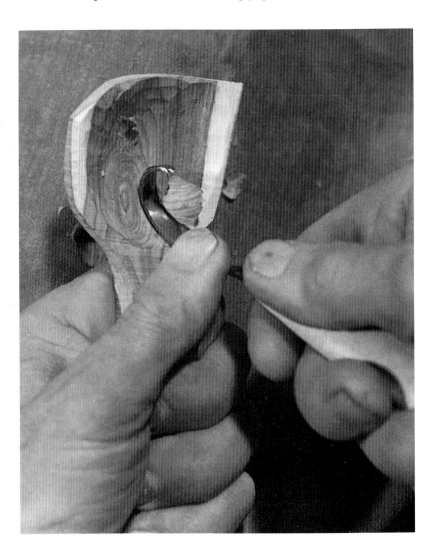

A single-edged carving hook makes it possible for the thumb to push, or be a fulcrum, for sweeping strokes that smoothly hollow a spoon bowl.

is cradled in the hand as you would hold a knife when using the draw grip. In this case, the side of the bowl becomes the steady rest for the thumb, which is important for both support and power. Shaving after shaving is rolled off the blank as the hook is squeezed toward the thumb. The blank is then reversed, and, working from the opposite side, the process is repeated.

A wrist grip works well with the carving hook, too. The top right photo shows a right-handed person using a right-edged hook. A left-handed person can use the same grip with a left-edged hook. The blank is locked on the knee with the opposite hand, and the ball of your carving hand's wrist serves as the fulcrum to lever the hook forward. Your elbow stays pressed against your side. You can also use your wrist as a fulcrum with a left-edged hook and lever toward yourself, as in the bottom right photo. You gain even more support and control by pressing your opposite thumb against your wrist. Notice how the hand stays in touch with the blank for support when using either of these grips.

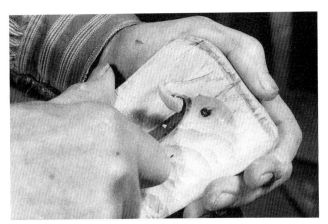

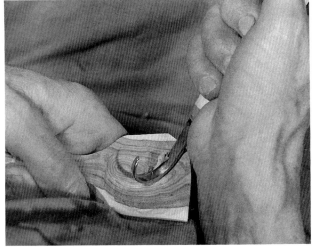

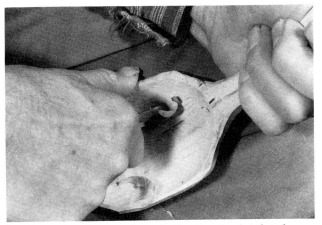

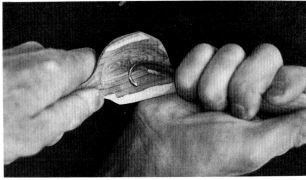

As shown in the top photo, hollowing the bowl is begun with a left-edged hook, using a draw grip. The other side of the bowl is worked using the same tool position, but the blank is reversed (bottom).

For a wrist grip, a right-handed person uses a right-edged hook, and levers the carving hook away from the body (top). A left-edged hook is used to lever the tool toward the body (bottom).

Hollowing with a gouge—Spoons, ladles and small bowls can be hollowed easily with a gouge. The advantage of the method described here is that it requires no holdfast clamping devices, so you can reposition the blank quickly and frequently. This is a safe way to work with a gouge, but it is imperative that you master the stops and the ways to support the blank. The carving technique is similar to that of other wrist grips. To learn the grips, study the pictures carefully. Turn the book upside down to observe the position of the hands as you would see your own.

A gouge with a deep sweep should be used for roughing out the bowl. Then switch to a gouge with a shallower sweep and remove the ridges left by the roughing gouge.

Grasp the blank from below and use a dagger grip on the gouge, flute-side up, as seen in the photo at left, below. The amount of shank sticking out of your hand should never exceed the width of the blank. You choke up on the gouge to make shorter strokes, as seen in the photo at right, below. The gouge hand uses the three fingers of the opposite hand for support and as a fulcrum. It is critical that you retain the support of those fingers, because they stop the gouge from following through into the opposite hand.

Press the thumb of your hand holding the blank against the flute of the gouge and the opposite hand to give support and control (top photo, facing page). When making certain strokes, it may feel better to move the thumb to the side of your hand or wrist. For support, your arms should be pressed against your sides and thighs. Keep your hands as close to each other as possible. Make the stroke with a scooping action across the grain. You rotate your wrist back and forth to take repeated strokes.

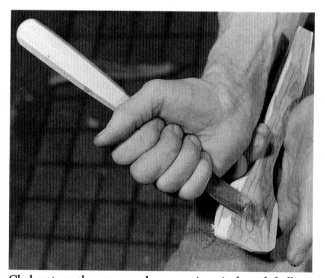

Choke up on the gouge and use a wrist grip for safe hollowing strokes.

With your arms pressed to your sides and your opposite thumb in the gouge flute, scooping strokes are made easy.

When you reverse the blank to work from the opposite side (bottom photo), grasp the blank between your thumb and index finger, curling your other fingers under the bowl for support. Use the same grip on the gouge as before, possibly choking up on it, to show less steel on the business end. Your stop is the edge of the blank. Your hand, not your wrist, should be firmly against it. Make short strokes from the beginning, using the same scooping action as earlier.

Continue repositioning the bowl and taking lighter cuts until you have a nicely sculpted hollow. You'll see it's quite easy to remove a lot of wood. In fact, you should be careful not to make your bowl too deep or too thin, especially if the front has end grain or slanting grain.

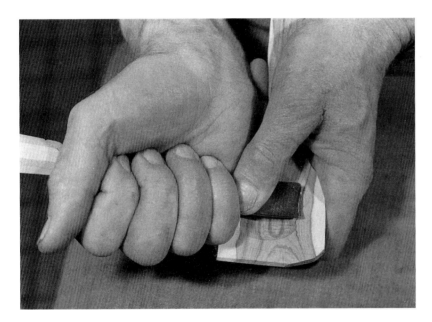

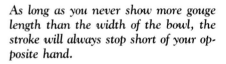

As long as you never show more gouge length than the width of the bowl, the stroke will always stop short of your opposite hand.

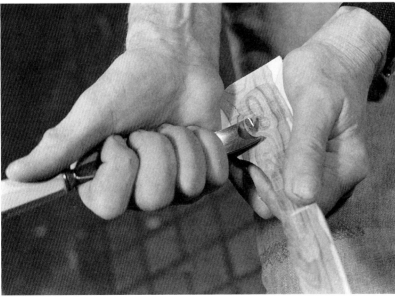

Working from the opposite side, hold the tool hand tightly against the blank.

Don't lose sight of the shape you want. A ladle should be capacious, but an eating spoon requires a relatively shallow bowl to feel right under your lip. It can be made deeper toward the back. Save enough wood along the back edge to be able to make final adjustments to the inside of the bowl later.

Drying the blank—If you are working with green wood, your blank must be dried before you can continue with final shaping and finish carving. Green wood carves easily, but it's fibrous, so when you try to smooth it, it tends to fray. Drying it makes it harder and crisp to cut. But you must take measures to keep the blank from drying too fast, which can cause it to check and crack.

Much of the rim can be smoothed with a draw grip (above). A thumb-joint grip will begin to go up-grain near the stem (facing page, left). To cut down-grain on the opposite edge, the ball of the wrist rests against the bowl's side, and the knife is pulled through the stroke by closing the hand (facing page, right).

I learned an excellent method at a workshop at the Sätergläntan School in 1974. The instructor, Birger Lindén, had carved a spoon from very green wood. It was evening. He rubbed its surface with a boiled potato and laid it on a warm radiator. The next morning the spoon was completely dry, without checks or cracks, and the potato didn't make further carving difficult.

Be particularly careful to rub the potato into the end-grain areas. The back of the bowl, both inside and out, should be given thorough attention, as well as the hook on a ladle. These are the thickest part of the spoon or ladle and they have exposed end grain on either side. If not retarded, moisture will leave these areas too quickly and cause checks and cracks.

Final shaping and smoothing—The rim of the bowl is usually the first area in need of attention. The draw grip can be used along most of it (see the photo on the facing page). But as you near the stem, you have to be careful of a change in grain direction. The photo at left, below shows a thumb-joint grip beginning to cut up-grain. A thumb-push stroke would reverse direction and help smooth the transition. To trim the opposite edge you can use a wrist grip (photo at right, below). The wrist or side of the hand gets support from the the rim of the bowl. The hand is opened and then closed to complete the stroke.

After you have finished trimming the upper edge of the bowl, examine it closely to detect any irregularities in the shape where it meets the rim. These can be corrected by reshaping the bowl with a carving hook or gouge.

Now shape the outside of the bowl so it follows the shape of the inside. Draw grips and thumb-joint grips reinforced with the fingers of

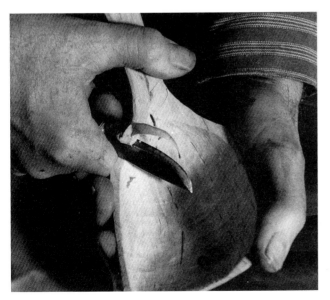

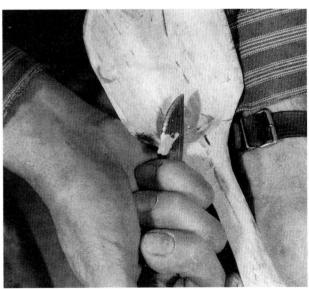

the opposite hand will give you the power you need to waste wood quickly on the back side. One side is easy, when you can support the stem against your body (top photo, below). When you switch to the opposite side you can use your thumb to press the blank into the opposite hand (bottom photo, below). Remember to leave the spine along the bowl bottom.

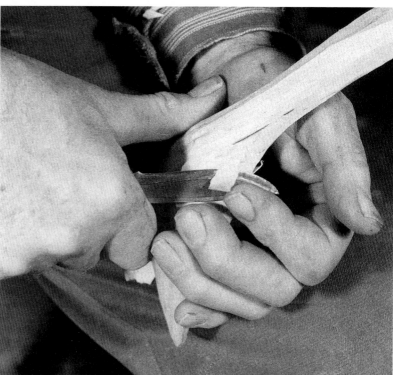

Reinforced thumb grips are used to thin the back of the bowl and the stem, sometimes carving across the grain. Remember to leave wood for the spine.

The photos below show the thumb-push stroke being used to shape various parts of the outside of the bowl. Use your fingers as calipers and check often to make certain the bowl isn't getting too thin. You can also hold the spoon up to a bright light to check for thin spots. It may be a good idea to mark them with a pencil to help you remember where they are.

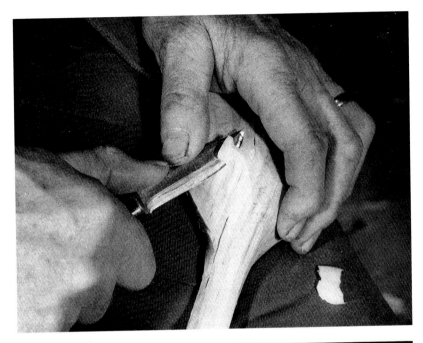

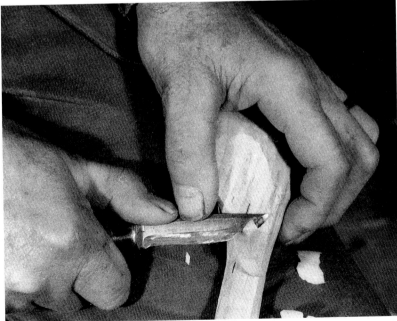

The blank is on the left knee and a thumb-push stroke smooths the transition from bowl to stem. Changes in grain direction in this area require frequent repositioning of the knife and blank.

A thumb-push stroke smoothes the back of the bowl toward the leading edge. Long strokes will leave a smooth surface.

Use your reference line to help you work out the final shape of the rest of the spoon. You can either judge the proportions by eye while carving, or draw them and then carve to the line. Your objective here is to refine the design of the spoon, defining the contours and smoothing the transitions between surfaces.

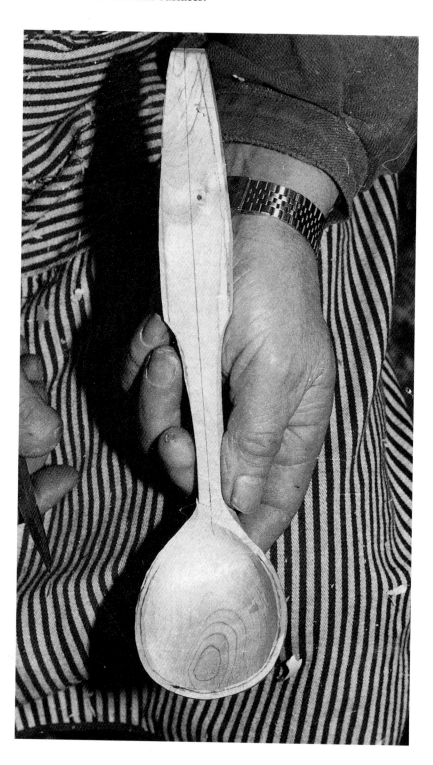

This dry ladle has its basic shape, and the pencil line identifies refinements yet to carve.

The photos below show the use of wrist grips, working outward and inward. In both cases, the carving hand gains support from the opposite hand. When doing the final carving it is important to have good control of movement at all times. Try to finish carve so it will be unnecessary to use abrasives to get the spoon smooth. Wooden surfaces cleaned up with sharp tools feel good to the touch. The alternative of using abrasives remains, if you are not satisfied when you are through with the knife work.

Smooth the stem with a wrist grip away from the body (left), and with the spoon reversed (right). Another wrist grip carves toward the body.

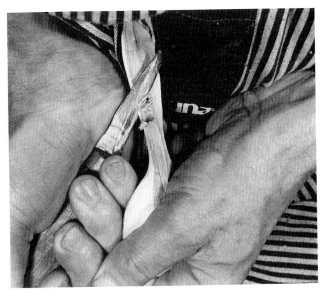
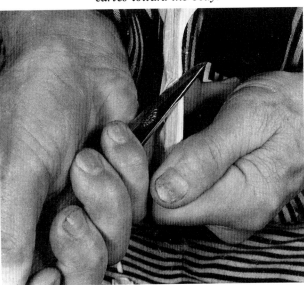

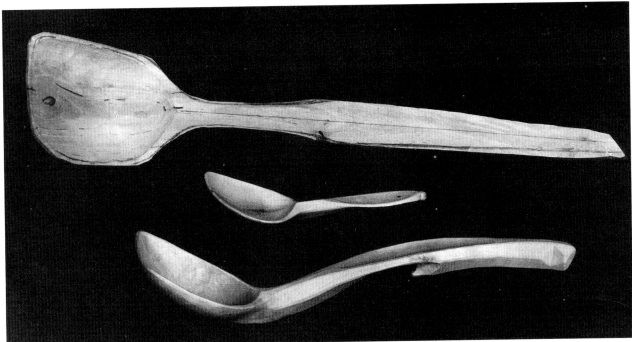

A roughed-out ladle after drying (top). The bold forms and lively textures of the spoon and ladle below it come from being finished without using sandpaper.

Finishing Touches

Sanding Before you begin sanding an object, be certain there is no further need to use edge tools on it. When you sand, grit fractures from the abrasive and lodges in the pores of the wood. Working with sharp tools on a sanded object will dull them quickly.

Sandpaper—I do not recommend the older types of sandpaper with sand or flint abrasives. These abrasives are not very hard and the grit does not adhere to the backing very well. Modern abrasives, such as Carborundum, aluminum oxide and silicone carbide, are far superior to older types.

Cloth-backed abrasives are the most expensive, but they're very wear-resistant. They are especially good for hand sanding because of their flexibility. Whatever sandpaper you choose, pieces 80mm by 50mm (3⅛ in. by 2 in.) are large enough for sanding utensils. It's a good idea to write the grit size on the back of the paper or store the pieces separately. When traveling, I keep my sandpaper in an easily sewn pouch bag, shown below.

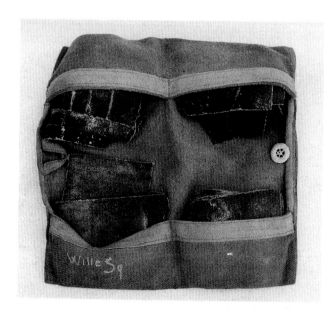

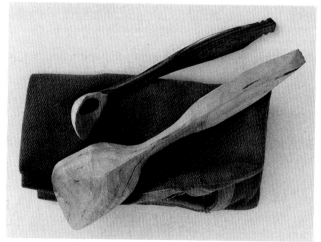

A pouch bag for storing abrasives (left), and the folded bag (above) with a marmalade spoon and a tablespoon ready for sanding.

When sanding by hand without a sanding block, it's a good idea to fold the sandpaper into thirds. Even small pieces should be folded this way because it gives you a good grip on them. There are basically two ways to hold the folded sandpaper. One edge can be pinched between your thumb and index finger, as shown in the top left photo below, or the sandpaper can be grasped between the joint of your thumb and the index finger, as in the bottom left photo. These grips can be varied in an unlimited number of ways.

Sanding techniques—Sanding is also shaping. A wooden object should be sanded as smooth as silk without losing its intended shape and sharpness of detail. Coarse sandpaper will quickly round edges, or worse, sand a hole in a thin spoon bowl. Don't blur the contour lines of your carving; use the sandpaper to straighten them and keep them crisp as you smooth the surface between them. This means you must often turn up an edge of the sandpaper to avoid rounding edges, as on the spoon bowl in the bottom right photo. Shape the sandpaper and, as much as possible, sand with the grain.

Don't skip sanding grits.

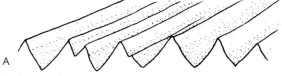

A
Surface sanded
with coarse sandpaper

B
*Fine abrasive smooths the surface,
without reaching the coarse scratches.*

Two basic grips for sandpaper, each with the folded cloth-backed abrasive between thumb and index finger.

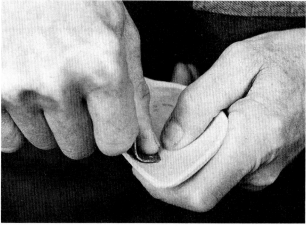

When sanding the bowl's inside, the edge of the sandpaper must be lifted slightly to avoid rounding the rim.

Your coarsest sandpaper will be the one you remove knife marks and unevenness with. Choose a grit no coarser than necessary to do the job efficiently. If the finish carving is done well, you can probably start with a grit of 100 or 120.

Don't be too hasty to make the transition from coarse to fine sandpaper. Go successively to finer grits, making certain all the scratches made by the preceding grit are gone before you switch to a finer paper. The drawing on the previous page shows an enlarged section of the ridges left by coarse sandpaper (A). After much sanding with a finer grit, the valleys still remain (B) because grits were skipped. Making the transition with several intermediate grits will make the sanding process quicker.

The direction from which light strikes the object you are sanding is very important. Diffused lighting or light striking a surface straight on, will make it difficult, if not impossible, to see scratches on the surface. Single-source, raking light, which is light from the side and down low, will accentuate detail and defects.

Final sanding—After sanding with the finest grit you intend to use, you should wet your spoon. Quickly flush it with water, or better yet, lukewarm water. This will raise the wood fibers on the surface. Let the spoon dry thoroughly. Use a fresh piece of 320-grit or finer sandpaper to sand the surface lightly. Stop when the surface is smooth. Continuing to sand will raise a new surface and new fibers, making it necessary to repeat the process.

Carved Engraving
When you have finished sanding your spoon, it's time to sign it by incising your initials on the back. A spoon with wood that lacks figure can be given more life by adding some ornamentation. Geometric designs can start with a simple reiteration of the outline of the handle and then be elaborated on. Fine sources of inspiration are arabesque and Viking ornamentation. If the spoon is meant to be a present, you may want to engrave a name and a date. Design the decorative pattern on a piece of paper first. You may have to make a number of drafts, letting your ideas mature, before you discover the right pattern.

I would like to coin the term *carved engraving* for the technique used here. Carved engraving is simply making a fine V cut along a line. The point of a knife makes the two angled cuts that meet to form the V. This technique is similar to chip carving. When signing and decorating spoons and utensils, the V lines should be so narrow that they are reminiscent of engraving. Real engraving is, of course, something completely different, where you use gravers or rotating burrs to cut into materials like stone, glass or metal. With those tools, however, you would never be able to attain sharp detail in wood or horn, and therefore you must use a knife.

Light is very important when you are engraving. If you are right-handed, the light should come from the left, and vice versa if you are left-handed. You need good eyesight, too. To be able to engrave, I must put a pair of magnifying glasses over my regular reading glasses.

Before you begin to engrave, you should lay out the letters or pattern on the object with a sharp pencil. To start with, you may even want to double the lines to show the actual thickness of the V line. If you don't have a special engraving knife (see p. 20), you can use your carving knife. It's a good idea to wrap the blade with masking tape, leaving only about 10mm (3/8 in.) of the tip exposed.

You need to have good control of the knife when you are engraving. It must not slip across the polished surface you are working on. One good way to hold a knife is to hold it like a pencil, with the blade and handle resting in the web of your thumb. The other hand holds the object, thumb on top, as close to the place you are engraving as possible. The thumb should be in back of the knife tip. You can use the thumb either to push the knife along its path or as a fulcrum, levering the handle of the knife toward your opposite hand. Both of these methods give you good control, and let you stop where you want to.

A pencil grip works fine for incising chips and making straight lines. Note how the thumb is used as a fulcrum to lever the knife tip.

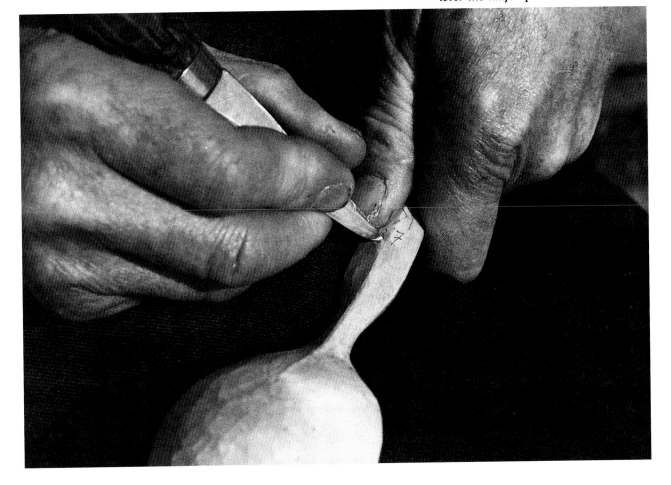

The first side of the V cut is made in one direction and the second from the opposite direction. Even here, it is important to cut down-grain, and not up into it. Don't angle the knife excessively. An angle of 70° to 75° is plenty. In some cases, you must make the cuts in the right order to avoid splitting out wood. For example, if you are going to engrave the letter N, make the two vertical lines first, then start each cut for the diagonal line at the end of each vertical line and cut toward the middle. If you fail to do so, you will risk splitting out the wood at the intersection between the diagonal lines and the vertical lines.

Engraving curved lines is difficult, but it can be done with practice. If you are making numbers like 0 or 8, you must make the inner cuts first to avoid splitting out the inner part of the circle. It is also possible to simplify curved lines by making several short straight lines. In some cases it may be impractical to use the thumb in back of the blade tip. Retaining the pencil grip, the knife can be pulled toward you as shown below. Notice how the opposite thumb gives support to the knife hand by applying pressure against the little finger's tip.

Finishing
Wooden spoons and ladles can be left unfinished. Dry, unfinished wood absorbs water like an ink blotter, and thus there is the possibility that a utensil could split or check if it dries quickly after being immersed in water. After being in use a long time, wooden utensils get a natural finish, because of the fats and oils they absorb. It's hard to retain the silky smooth texture that remains after the final sanding, but in time the utensils will gain their own patina.

An old recipe for finishing cooking utensils is merely to boil them in milk for a couple of hours. The casein, which is sometimes used in water-resistant cold-water paint or glue, is absorbed into the wood, protecting and preserving it.

When carving toward you, which is often necessary in tracing curved lines, use the thumb of your opposite hand to brace the little finger of your knife hand.

Vegetable oil or liquid paraffin (not British paraffin, which is kerosene) can be used to treat wooden utensils. Vegetable oil is not very good, though, because it can become rancid. On the other hand, liquid paraffin is tasteless and odorless. But neither of these oils will cure. They will be absorbed by the wood and thicken somewhat, but never really dry. The surface of the wood doesn't harden from them, and after washing many times, the wood becomes grayish.

A short-handled, straight-edged engraving knife. The butt can be nestled in the web of the thumb and index finger.

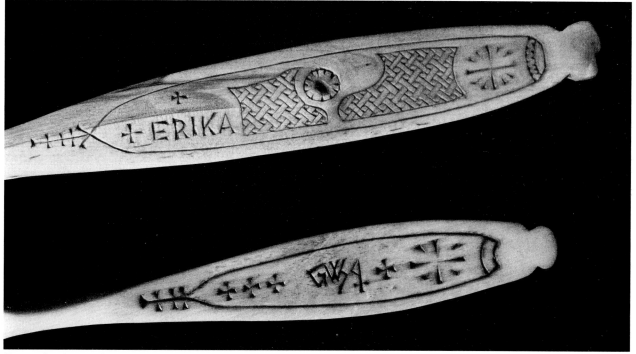

Personalized spoon handles with carved engravings. Notice how the knot in the top spoon has been integrated into the design.

Raw linseed oil is a better alternative to vegetable oil or liquid paraffin. It is transparent, nontoxic and so clean that it can be used in cooking. Its disadvantage is that it takes a long time to cure—a half year or so at room temperature. It will soak deeply into the wood, and therefore I would recommend that it be applied two or three times, with about a week between applications. Small utensils can be soaked in the oil. Soaking should saturate the wood. To prevent oil buildup on the surface, wipe off any remaining oil. A cured oil skin is difficult to remove by sanding. Raw linseed oil can usually be found in art-supply, hardware and some natural-food stores.

Another nontoxic oil that cures is walnut oil. It is edible and is sold in health-food stores. Apply walnut oil as you would raw linseed oil. Its curing time is about the same as for raw linseed oil, but the process can be accelerated by heating the oil in a double boiler or by immersing the oil container in water that is already hot. The latter is safer, especially if your source of heat is gas. If you do choose to heat the oil on the stove, you should have a cover handy to snuff out the fire should the oil ignite.

Applying a finish on wood always raises the fibers somewhat, and oils are no exception. Therefore, it is necessary to resand your utensils after oiling. Use the same type of oil, applying it to both the sandpaper (320 grit to 400 grit) and the utensil, then wet sand. Dry sanding is not recommended because the abrasive will be quickly clogged by the cured oil. Wipe afterwards with paper toweling or a clean cloth. You will now have a silky smooth surface that will be able to withstand wear and washing. It's not a good idea to let wooden utensils soak in the dishpan, and you should not wash them in a dishwasher. Air drying them is fine.

Boiled linseed oil is excellent for finishing carved objects other than those that come into contact with food. Boiled linseed oil contains heavy-metal driers and is poisonous. It cures within a couple of weeks, but the heavy metals can leach from the surface. To increase its absorption into wood, you can thin it with turpentine spirits. A mixture for the first application should be about one part turpentine to two parts oil. Repeat the process after a few days using a mixture with 10% turpentine spirits or just the oil. Boiled linseed oil can be also used without thinners, even for the first application. It leaves a yellowish hue on light-colored woods.

Caution: Spontaneous combustion can occur in rags and paper saturated with linseed oil. There is even a greater danger of this happening if the oil is full of dust. Store rags or paper saturated with linseed oil in a metal container with an airtight lid, or dispose of them by burning in a safe place. Keep them submerged in water until disposal.

Using Wood

Finding and Using Wood The wood you choose when you want to begin carving depends on what you want to carve. Some carvers like to start out by practicing grips and techniques on scrap wood; others prefer to start on a usable article.

One of the easiest materials to carve with a knife is thick pine bark. Pine bark can be used to carve boats, animals and other figures. It is a fine material to start with, especially for children. Alder, basswood and sugar pine are easy woods to carve because they are close grained but not too hard. Cottonwood and willow are loose and porous, while aspen is somewhat denser. All these species are good for bowls, dough bowls and platters. In Sweden, aspen is the most common wood for dough bowls. In recent years, a wood called jelutong has found its way into school shops. This wood is very porous and easy to carve, but it's expensive. It is also an allergen.

Wood for spoons and ladles—Wood for spoons and ladles should be strong and hard, fairly dense and close grained. Birch, maple, hornbeam, beech, sorb, mountain ash, bird cherry, dogwood and hawthorn are excellent woods for spoons and ladles. Most fruitwood, such as apple, pear, plum and cherry, is also fine. Apple is especially good because apple trees usually have many natural crooks. Small spoons can be made from the dense and tough wood found in many shrubs, such as lilac, laurel, rhododendron and Russian olive.

Many of these woods are often found close to buildings or on older lots. Always ask for the owner's permission before you harvest a tree. Permission is necessary even if you are deep in the forest and are interested in a very common tree. Letting friends and neighbors know what you are looking for is another good way to get wood. They may save prunings for you, or let you know if they decide to remove a tree from their property. A few will even want to know how they should care for the wood. I usually just ask them to store it in a cool, shady place, or sometimes hint that sealing the end grain with white or yellow glue or some latex paint will help keep the wood from checking.

If you are satisfied working with straight-grained wood, or if you don't have a choice, you can buy birch or maple at most lumberyards. For other hardwoods and more exotic woods, you will have to find dealers who supply them.

Harvesting trees—If you have the possibility of deciding for yourself, the best time to harvest trees is in the late fall. This is the time of the year when the trees contain the least amount of water; they are relatively dormant between growth periods. In addition, you have the whole winter ahead of you for the wood to begin drying. Even if winters are drier than summers, the fact that there is less water in the wood retards its tendency to check or crack.

I have heard of other times that were deemed best for harvesting trees, and I will relate the following from an old book called *Crafts and Craftsmanship (Slöjd och Handverk)*, in a chapter entitled "Ladle-material-cutting day." According to the book, the best day of the year to collect ladle blanks is the the 19th of March, which is the Swedish name day celebrating Joseph. That particular day was probably chosen because Joseph, father of Jesus, was a carpenter. It was believed that Jesus blessed the material gathered on that day. Food that was stirred and served with a ladle taken on that day would be nutritious and satisfying, and could be stored for a long time without spoiling.

Preventing checks and cracks—Wood would not be so complicated if it shrank equally in all directions. This, however, is not the case. Longitudinal shrinkage is minimal and, with a few exceptions, doesn't have to be taken into consideration. Most people know that a board shrinks across its width, but many are not aware of the fact that as wood dries, it shrinks in a rather complicated and uneven order. The unevenness creates stress, and the stress is relieved in checking and cracking. So the trick is to minimize the stress.

Splitting and sawing round stock down the center of the pith will relieve much of the stress that develops in wood when it dries. The blank can now change shape without cracking apart. Also, it is smaller in section, and since wood dries from the outside in, the smaller the section, the more evenly it will dry. This is also why one of the best methods for preventing checking and cracking in wood for carving is to rough out blanks when the wood is green. Often this is not possible, and wood will have to be stored and dried. Now the task is to control the drying so that tension is not created between the drier, shrinking outside and the relatively wet inside.

Sealing the end grain as soon as possible after cutting the stock is an important measure for inhibiting checks. In dry weather during spring and summer, end checking can start within a few minutes after you have felled a tree. There are commercial sealers for this specific purpose, but you can make do with yellow or white glue, or even leftover water-based paints.

Green wood should be stored in a cool, damp place, in the shade and under cover. Use scrap stock or make some other provision to keep it off the ground and separated. If you cover it with plastic film or a tarp to keep the rain off, leave the pile open on the sides for air circulation. Not doing so would invite fungus and insect damage. Under a roof overhang on the north side of a shed or barn is a good place to start drying wood. It can later be moved inside a shed or other building that will permit outside-air circulation.

How long wood should be air dried outdoors will vary with the kind of wood, its thickness, the amount of bark left on it and the average humidity during its drying period. This could be a matter of weeks for thin debarked wood or boards, or years for thick timbers and round stock. Birch and bird cherry will quickly become tainted and start to rot if the bark is not at least partially removed. Willow, on the other hand, can be left with the bark on for two or three years without rotting, but it will not dry very much during that time.

The transition from outside air to the inside climate of the house or shop is perhaps the most drastic change that wood goes through in the drying process. If possible, this transition should be made during the summer months of the year. This is especially the case if you are moving thick pieces of wood indoors. The warm, dry indoor air during the winter heating season will speed the drying process and increase the stresses on the wood. This problem, however, will be minimal when dealing with small pieces of wood for things like utensils. In this case, it is not necessary, or even advisable, to dry or store the wood in heated buildings. Wood is easier to carve when it is not completely dry. Seasoned wood can be dampened to make it easier to carve. Dried burls for bowls are sometimes even boiled for this reason.

Drying green-wood blanks—It is very simple to rough out blanks in green wood. Many people believe that doing this will make it almost impossible to dry them without the development of checks and cracks. This is definitely not true. The larger the mass of wood, the harder it is to dry. Spoon and ladle blanks are very thin, and therefore easy to dry without cracking.

The drying process should be started in a cool, damp place: in a cellar or on the north side of a shed, out of the sun. Even still, some measure should be taken to slow the initial drying. One good way is to rub a boiled potato into the blank. Oil is not a good alternative if the blank is to be sanded later because the oil will clog the sandpaper.

Blanks can be buried in sawdust or shavings, or wrapped with newspapers and kept in plastic bags. If you use newspapers, change them every day for the first few days. A disadvantage of the plastic-bag method is that mold will often develop on the blanks. Both of these methods work because moisture migrates more slowly into sawdust or newspapers than into circulating air.

Sources
of Supply

*These mail-order houses can provide most edge tools
and sharpening supplies:*

Country Workshops
(for specialty tools)
90 Mill Creek Road
Marshall, NC 27853
(704) 656-2280

Fine Tool Shops
170 West Road
P.O. Box 7091
Portsmouth, NH 03801
(603) 433-0409

Frog Tool Co. Ltd.
700 W. Jackson Boulevard
Chicago, IL 60606
(312) 648-1270
West of the Rocky Mountains:
P.O. Box U
Ventura, CA 93002

Garrett Wade
161 Avenue of the Americas
New York, NY 10013-1205
(800) 221-2942
(212) 807-1757 in New York

Grieger's, Inc.
(for abrasive grits)
900 S. Arroyo Parkway
Bin 41
Pasadena, CA 91109
(818) 795-9775

Highland Hardware
1045 N. Highland Avenue, N.E.
Atlanta, Georgia 30306
(404) 872-4466

Lee Valley Tools
1080 Morrison Drive
Ottawa, Ontario
Canada K2H 8K7
(613) 596-0350

McMaster-Carr Supply
(for grindstones)
Box 4355
Chicago, IL 60680
(312) 834-9600

Sarjent Tools Ltd.
44-52 Oxford Road
Reading, Berkshire
RG1 7LH
England

Woodcraft
41 Atlantic Avenue
10 State Street
Box 4000
Woburn, MA 01888
(800) 225-1153
(617) 935-5860 in
Massachusetts

Editors: Rick Mastelli, James Rudström
Designer: Deborah Fillion
Layout artist: Henry Roth
Copy/production editor: Pam Purrone
Art assistant: Iliana Koehler
Typesetter: Nancy Knapp
Print production manager: Peggy Dutton

Typeface: ITC Goudy
Paper: Warrenflo, 70 lb., neutral pH
Printer and binder: Ringier, Olathe, Kansas

If you've enjoyed Wille Sundqvist's book, you won't want to miss his son's video.

The rich tradition of Swedish woodworking comes alive in video. Wille's son, Jögge, demonstrates how to make a dough bowl and a spoon from start to finish. He shows you the grips, strokes and rhythms that make for successful carving. And like his father in the book, Jögge explores the fundamentals of good design. 60 minutes

To order *Carving Swedish Woodenware with Jögge Sundqvist*, just fill out this card and send your payment of $29.95, plus $2.50 postage and handling (CT residents add 8% sales tax), to the address below.

Check one ☐ VHS (060035) ☐ Beta (060036)

Name _____

Address _____

City _____ State _____ Zip _____

☐ My payment is enclosed ☐ MasterCard ☐ VISA ☐ American Express

Charge Card # _____

Expiration Date _____

Signature _____

TAUNTON BOOKS & VIDEOS

...by fellow enthusiasts

The Taunton Press, 63 South Main St., Box 5506, Newtown, CT 06470-5506 1-800-888-8286.

For more information...

We hope you enjoy this book and find it useful in your work. If you would like to know more about *Fine Woodworking* magazine and Taunton Press books and videos, just fill out this card and return it to us.

Name _____

Address _____

City _____ State _____ Zip _____

I'm interested in:
☐ building and remodeling
☐ gardening and landscaping
☐ woodworking and cabinetmaking
☐ sewing, knitting and needlecrafts